CORNELL STUDIES IN CIVIL LIBERTY

Tenure in American Higher Education:
Plans, Practices, and the Law

TENURE IN AMERICAN HIGHER EDUCATION:
Plans, Practices, and the Law

◇◇

By **CLARK BYSE**

Law School of Harvard University

and **LOUIS JOUGHIN**

American Association of University Professors

CORNELL UNIVERSITY PRESS

Ithaca, New York

PRINTED IN THE UNITED STATES OF AMERICA BY THE

VAIL-BALLOU PRESS, INC., BINGHAMTON, NEW YORK

Foreword

SELDOM does a book fill a more important need than this admirable study of academic tenure and related subjects by Clark Byse and Louis Joughin. Old and widely accepted as is the basic concept that faculty members who have served a proper period of apprenticeship shall enjoy security in their posts and be subject to removal only for "adequate cause," this is the first attempt to subject this important aspect of academic life to systematic analysis. Moreover, the timing of the book's appearance could not be better. American higher education is just emerging from a difficult postwar period in which academic freedom, academic tenure, and academic due process have fared quite badly and in which the administrative officers and governing boards of a good many institutions of higher learning have shown an alarming tendency to sacrifice essential aspects of the academic way of life to the crass pressures of power-hungry politicians and "know-nothing" elements of the public. The momentary calm that has followed the shameful excesses of the McCarthy Era supplies faculty members, administrative officers, governing boards, and the public alike with an excellent opportunity to achieve a better understanding of the basic principles that must govern research and teaching in a free society and, above all, of the concept of a "university." As surely as the sun rises and sets, new threats to these fundamental aspects of the liberal, democratic way of life will arise. It is to be hoped that, when this happens, our society will be better prepared to resist unprincipled attacks upon institutions of higher learning and their faculties than it was during the years just past.

One is entitled to hope that we have all learned something by experience and that even on a pragmatic basis we would "do better" next time. But there is still a pressing need for carefully organized, readily accessible formulations of the basic traditions and principles of academic freedom, tenure, and due process. This present book by Messrs. Byse and Joughin goes far toward meeting this need.

Even though it enjoys a venerable tradition, academic tenure is a much-misunderstood aspect of American higher education. For one thing, contrary to popular belief, a professor seldom acquires tenure automatically. He must first survive a long and exacting training for his profession in which many candidates fall by the wayside. Under any of the systems now in use by colleges and universities, or recommended by such educational organizations as the American Association of University Professors or the Association of American Colleges, he then serves a testing period on the job. At the end of this period the administrative officers of his institution and his academic peers consciously and formally pass judgment upon him and determine whether he shall be appointed to a faculty post without limit of time or be sent on his way. Messrs. Byse and

Joughin admirably state the rationale that justifies this system by which a tested scholar is allowed to follow a courageous, enterprising career, free from the threat of dismissal merely because some superior may dislike him or the results of his scholarship.

It is proper to stress here the little-recognized fact that "tenure" is a widely accepted aspect of employment in many areas other than the academic one. It often passes unchallenged, and even unrecognized, in such diverse occupational fields as business, the law, religion, and the civil service. The very college and university trustees who so often rail against this system that "freezes the professor into his job" are themselves frequently the beneficiaries of a tenure system, for many an institution makes use of "life trustees." There is also the ready analogy of the federal judge who holds office "for life during good behavior." The reasons that led the Founding Fathers thus to prescribe a tenure system for judges in 1787 and the way in which the system has operated in the ensuing century and three-quarters have much in common with the pattern of tenure in academic life. Indeed, judicial tenure is the more binding type, for the academic profession accepts the principle of automatic retirement because of age—often as early as sixty-five and almost never later than seventy—whereas federal judges are allowed to, and frequently do, "die with their boots on."

Thus the common notion that the college professor, almost alone among professional men, is "frozen into" his post simply is not in accordance with the facts of life. Moreover, it is important to note that the academic profession itself readily concedes that a professor can be dismissed for "adequate cause," including such grounds as incompetence, neglect of duty, and gross personal misconduct. If not as many professors are dismissed for these reasons as some may deem desirable, again it is well to remember that in such fields as the law, the ministry, and many areas of business, justice is also frequently tempered with mercy in dealing with incompetent or neglectful people.

The record of recent years reveals that more than one institution of higher learning, presumably committed to academic tenure, has gone badly astray when it has found itself compelled to come to grips with a dismissal case. Sometimes the trouble has been the absence of clear-cut institutional regulations prescribing the procedures to be followed in such a case. Sometimes it has been failure to adhere to these regulations, particularly in the absence of any experience under them in earlier cases. A dismissal proceeding in a well-run university is in the nature of things a rather rare event. Perhaps it was for this reason that even so respected an educational leader as A. Lawrence Lowell was guilty of such foolish words as the following: "Tradition has great advantages over regulations. It is a more delicate instrument: it accommodates itself to things which are not susceptible of sharp definition: it is more flexible in its application." Maybe so. But if "tradition" rather than "regulations" can be depended on to safeguard the individual in all of his procedural dealings with authority, seven centuries of effort since Magna Carta to compel public officers to deal with private persons in accordance with "the law of the land" have been curiously misguided. Clearly President Lowell was wrong in his belief that "regulations" are inferior to "tradition" in academic proceedings, and Messrs. Byse and Joughin are right when they observe that "academic government no less than political government must contain safeguards against human frailty." Fortunately there is now available to American institutions of higher learning a model code of academic due process regulations in a statement published in 1958 under the joint auspices of the Association of American Colleges and the American Association of University Professors. The text of this code is printed as an appendix to the present book.

Not the least of the merits of Messrs. Byse and Joughin's volume is its perceptive examination of the difficult relationship that exists between trustees and faculty members in many American institutions of higher learning. The members of a university governing board, typically the agents of the dominant social groups in the community, are very likely to be concerned about the *conservation* of established values and institutions. Teachers and research scholars, on the other hand, have the historic duty "to follow the argument wherever it may lead," with the natural result that academic men are often somewhat more interested in effecting change than in preserving the *status quo*. There is thus something of a built-in source of antagonism between trustees and teachers in academic life, and it is essential that each group understand the other's role and responsibilities if a university is to be a healthy place. To put it differently, the various components that make up a university's organization and purpose must be brought into some sort of reasonable balance. Messrs. Byse and Joughin properly suggest that the balance is presently a bit askew in many an institution—askew to the disadvantage of faculties. There is more than a little bite in their wry observation that, while the means are readily available in most universities whereby trustees can undertake to get rid of a teacher, there is virtually no institution in the land that invites its faculty to challenge an incompetent trustee's right to continue in his post.

Another point effectively made in the following pages is that the academic profession must take a bolder line of action in cases in which teachers have been improperly dismissed. The American Association of University Professors has made many admirable investigations of dismissal cases, and the resulting reports have effectively demonstrated the degree to which certain institutions have departed from sound tenure and dismissal standards. But it has to be sadly confessed that it is virtually impossible to point to a case in which such activity by the profession has resulted in the reinstatement of a teacher deemed to have been wrongly dismissed. The curt advice of this book that "the remedy for infringement of tenure should include an order of reinstatement" should be promptly and vigorously followed by the profession.

One of the most valuable features of this book is its systematic evaluation of the treatment academic freedom and academic tenure have received in the courts. The authors make clear their personal belief that a college or university's regulations on these subjects should create a contractual relationship between professor and institution enforceable in the courts. Some members of the profession may have misgivings about such dependence upon the courts for the clarification and enforcement of academic regulations. While there are occasional outstanding examples of excellent judicial rulings in support of academic tenure, the record reveals that the great majority of American judges, state and federal alike, have up to now shared with much of the public many serious misconceptions of the meaning and purpose of academic freedom and tenure. Just recently the Supreme Court of South Dakota, in sustaining the dismissal of a professor with tenure from South Dakota State College, without charges or a hearing, paid its respects to academic tenure in these dubious terms: "The exact meaning and intent of this so-called tenure policy eludes us. Its vaporous objectives, purposes, and procedures are lost in a fog of nebulous verbiage."

Members of the profession will want to ponder carefully the very persuasive case set forth in these pages for the making of vigorous efforts by the academic profession to overcome this kind of judicial attitude and to secure court enforcement of the accepted standards of academic life. At the time this is written, the American Association of University Professors has submitted an *amicus curiae* brief to the United States Supreme Court in a case in which there was an academic freedom element, and it is giving careful thought to similar action in other cases. At the same time, the Association is proceeding slowly in this direction and is governed by a proper sense of caution. There is much to be said for the position that the standards governing higher education—including the rules of academic freedom, tenure, and due process—can best be worked out on a private, voluntary basis by teachers, administrative officers, trustees, and organizations representing these groups. In particular, if universities can be persuaded to allow dismissal cases to be tried before all-faculty tribunals with a commitment on the part of governing boards to accept the recommendations of these tribunals in all but the most unusual cases, there will be little reason for either side in such proceedings to resort to the courts on appeal.

Messrs. Byse and Joughin have written a book that has

many levels of merit, a book that will be useful to different groups of people in different ways. Teachers, administrative officers, and trustees at institutions that are endeavoring to perfect their own tenure regulations will find very useful the wealth of information in these pages about the practices, both good and bad, that are followed at other institutions. Similarly, the authors' own recommendations embodied in Chapter IV, as well as those in the documents printed in the Appendices, supply excellent blueprints for further action at these institutions. Judges and lawyers can derive valuable guidance from the book's third chapter in their further efforts to clarify the law of tenure with respect to both public institutions operating under general constitutional or legislative mandates and private institutions that are less rigidly bound by such legal mandates but are often prone to let important professional relationships rest upon informal bases. Finally the observations set forth in the concluding chapter concerning the status of the academic profession in a democratic society, although brief and tentative, raise some provocative questions about the present uneasy peace that prevails between the goals and standards of the academic profession and the purposes and values of our business society. It is no mere cliché to say that American higher education is at the crossroads. The way ahead is bound to be difficult at best. With respect to troublesome issues in the areas of academic freedom, tenure, and due process, we can do a lot worse than to follow the advice set forth in these pages.

ROBERT K. CARR
Joel Parker Professor of Law and Political Science,
Dartmouth College;
Chairman, Committee A on Academic Freedom and
Tenure, American Association of University Professors

Preface

THIS study was undertaken for the American Academic Freedom Project at Columbia University and was financed by a grant from the Fund for the Republic. Neither the Project nor the Fund exercised supervision or control, and thus neither is in any way responsible for the interpretations and views here presented.

We are grateful to the Project and the Fund for making the study possible. We also wish to express our appreciation to the presidents and other administrators, as well as faculty members—usually officers of local chapters of the American Association of University Professors—who responded to our requests for information. Our thanks also go to Meyer Kramer and Ronald Wertheim for legal research assistance and to Mrs. Maury Soltes for preparation of the Index.

Chapter II, "Plans and Practices," was written by Mr. Joughin, and Chapter III, "Tenure and the Law," by Mr. Byse. The introductory comments of Chapter I and the conclusions and recommendations of Chapter IV are of joint authorship.

CLARK BYSE

LOUIS JOUGHIN

March, 1959

xiii

Contents

Tenure in American Higher Education:
Plans, Practices, and the Law

I

Introduction

THIS study provides information and appraisal about the acquisition and termination of tenure in American colleges and universities—examining particularly the roles of governing boards, administrative officials, and faculties in those areas of decision and discussing the role of the courts in enforcing the tenure principle.

The most widely accepted statement of academic tenure —that of the Association of American Colleges and the American Association of University Professors—provides, "After the expiration of a probationary period teachers or investigators should have permanent or continuous tenure, and their services should be terminated only for adequate cause, except in the case of retirement for age, or under extraordinary circumstances because of financial exigencies." [1] As will be developed, there are many variations and

[1] 1940 "Statement of Principles" on "Academic Freedom and Tenure" originally formulated and endorsed by the American Association of University Professors and the Association of American

modifications. But the essential characteristic of tenure as the term is here employed is continuity of service, in that the institution in which the teacher serves has in some manner—either as a legal obligation or as a moral commitment—relinquished the freedom or power it otherwise would possess to terminate the teacher's services.[2]

The principal justification for academic tenure is that it enables a faculty member to teach, study, and act free from a large number of restraints and pressures which otherwise would inhibit independent thought and action.[3] This justification of freedom for teachers, customarily termed "academic freedom," is similar to that which accounts for the proscription in the Bill of Rights of governmental interference with the citizen's general freedoms of thought and expression. These general freedoms exist both because of the moral conviction that the political state should not limit the individual's inalienable rights of life and liberty and because of the pragmatic recognition that free trade in ideas is an indispensable condition to enlightened community decision and action.[4]

Colleges; and later adopted by a number of other organizations. See *AAUP Bulletin* 44: 290–293 (1958). The "Statement" is reprinted here, for ready reference, in Appendix C.

[2] Security against dismissal may be for a fixed term, or for the professional life of the teacher; in the former case the tenure is "limited," in the latter it is "indefinite," "continuous," or "permanent."

[3] See the thoughtful paper of Professor Edwin O. Stene for discussion of other justifications of academic tenure, "Bases of Academic Tenure," *AAUP Bulletin* 41: 584–589 (1955).

[4] Henry Steele Commager, *Freedom, Loyalty, Dissent* (1954), ch. 1. Recall John Stuart Mill's classic expression in his essay *On Liberty:* "The peculiar evil of silencing the expression of an opinion is, that it is robbing the human race; posterity as well as the

INTRODUCTION

But there is more to academic freedom. Teachers in colleges and universities in our society have the unique responsibility to help students to develop critical capacities.
Teachers must also strive to make available the accumu-
lated knowledge of the past, to expand the frontiers of
knowledge, to appraise existing institutions, and to seek
their correction or replacement in the light of reason and
experience. If they are to perform these indispensable
tasks, there must be free inquiry and discussion. This, as
Professor Fritz Machlup has noted, demands more than
mere "absence of governmental sanctions, more than a
guarantee that . . . [professors] will not be jailed for the
expressions of their thoughts. If they are to be encouraged
to pursue the truth wherever it may lead, to 'follow out
any bold, vigorous, independent train of thought . . . ,'
they need protection from all more material sanctions, especially from dismissal." [5] Professor Machlup continues:

With regard to some occupations, it is eminently in the interest of society that men concerned speak their minds without
fear of retribution. . . . The occupational work of the vast
majority of people is largely independent of their thought and
speech. The professor's work *consists* of his thought and
speech. If he loses his position for what he writes or says, he
will, as a rule, have to leave his profession, and may no longer

existing generation; those who dissent from the opinion, still more
than those who hold it. If the opinion is right, they are deprived
of the opportunity of exchanging error for truth; if wrong, they
lose, what is almost as great a benefit, the clearer perception and
livelier impression of truth, produced by its collision with error."
Mill, *Utilitarianism, Liberty, and Representative Government* (Ev-
eryman's Library, ed. Rhys.), 79.
  [5] Fritz Machlup, "On Some Misconceptions Concerning Academic Freedom," *AAUP Bulletin* 41: 753, 755-756 (1955).

3

TENURE IN AMERICAN HIGHER EDUCATION

be able effectively to question and challenge accepted doctrines. And if *some* professors lose their positions for what they write or say, the effect on many other professors will be such that their usefulness to their students and to society will be gravely reduced.[6]

The lasting damage brought about by infringements of academic freedom and tenure thus is not only to the very small group of teachers directly affected. It is also to society as a whole, because the ultimate beneficiaries of academic freedom are not those who exercise it but all the people. This deserves emphasis: Academic freedom and tenure do not exist because of a peculiar solicitude for the human beings who staff our academic institutions. They exist, instead, in order that society may have the benefit of honest judgment and independent criticism which otherwise might be withheld because of fear of offending a dominant social group or transient social attitude.

A helpful analogy may be found in what may be termed "judicial freedom" and tenure. The Constitution provides, "The Judges, both of the supreme and inferior courts, shall hold their Offices during good behavior, and shall, at stated Times, receive for their services, a Compensation which shall not be diminished during their continuance in office."[7] The standard "of good behavior for the continuance in office," Hamilton wrote, "is the best expedient which can be devised in any government, to secure a steady, upright, and impartial administration of the laws."[8] Such a standard for continued employment of teachers in colleges and universities similarly provides the best safeguard from re-

[6] *Ibid.*, 756.
[7] Art. III, § 1, U.S. Constitution.
[8] *The Federalist*, No. 78. In No. 79 Hamilton stressed that "a power over a man's subsistence amounts to a power over his will."

4

straints and pressures which otherwise might deter a "steady, upright, and impartial" performance of the teacher's indispensable task of critical thought and analysis.[9]

Perhaps a caveat is necessary. Despite the unquestioned importance of tenure, like most institutions of a free society, it can be misused. Tenure can become an instrument to perpetuate incompetence and mediocrity rather than to advance scholarship and talent. But the fact that tenure can be debased does not mean that it is less valuable. It means only that other processes must not be neglected—including careful selection of those to whom tenure is awarded and courageous action by administrators and faculty to weed out those who thereafter become professionally unfit.

In the United States the significance of academic freedom is understood by virtually all teachers in higher education. Many informed members of the general public are in agreement. Particularly, it is clear that numerous trustees and administrators enthusiastically support the freedom of teachers, because they well understand that such freedom is one of the chief positive forces at work in their institutions. Unfortunately, however, there are problems. Principle is not everywhere supported by adequate practice; the legal basis is by no means satisfactory; and in some institutions the concept of tenure which supports the freedom of the teacher is so poorly developed as to suggest indifference or even hostility on the part of trustees and administrators.

It is our hope that this study, by providing information, analysis, and recommendations concerning the acquisition

[9] And see Zechariah Chafee, Jr., *The Blessings of Liberty* (1956), 241: "The government pays judges but it does not tell them how to decide. An independent . . . university is as essential to the community as an independent judiciary."

and termination of tenure, will stimulate critical self-examination by governing boards, administrative officials, and faculties—the three groups most intimately concerned. Considerations of time and money made it necessary to limit the survey of plans and practices to higher education in California, Illinois, and Pennsylvania (states selected because of the number and variety of their institutions). But the representative character of the institutions surveyed, the fact that the legal discussion touches on cases in other states, and the general applicability of the conclusions and recommendations should give the report significance for colleges and universities throughout the country.

The study is primarily based on the tenure plans and questionnaire replies supplied by eighty institutions, which are listed in Appendix A. The questionnaire, reproduced in Appendix B, was sent to the 352 institutions of higher education in California, Illinois, and Pennsylvania listed in the *Education Directory, 1954–55, Part 3* (U.S. Department of Health, Education, and Welfare; Office of Education, 1955).[10] The response was as follows:

	Reply	*No reply* [11]	*Total*
California	74 (55%)	60 (45%)	134 (100%)
Illinois	42 (41%)	61 (59%)	103 (100%)
Pennsylvania	54 (47%)	61 (53%)	115 (100%)
Total	170 (48%)	182 (52%)	352 (100%)

[10] The questionnaire was mailed out in June, 1955; replies were received through October, 1955; the choice of institutions to be studied was then made, and November, 1955, became the "cut-off date." Miscellaneous questions relating to fact and interpretation were sent to the selected institutions and other persons in 1956. The first draft of the text was mailed to the co-operating colleges and universities in April, 1957, for correction and comment.

[11] Including three refusals and seven replies promised but not received.

In the three states most of the institutions which would generally be regarded as of major stature replied. The eighty institutions included in the study were selected by a process of exclusion from the one hundred and seventy which answered. Those excluded were state teachers colleges, junior colleges, and institutions of specialized interest (such as aeronautical schools and colleges of optometry) which appear to be staffed largely by part-time personnel who have another status as practicing professionals. These institutions were not excluded because their tenure practices do not deserve study, for the opposite is true. Rather, the decision not to include them was based on our belief that within the limits of the time and effort we could devote to the subject it was better to deal intensively with the older and more traditional institutions of higher learning rather than cursorily with the more diverse grouping.[12] Thus the study focuses on the tenure plans and practices of so-called "private" colleges, although three state-financed universities are also included.

After the report was prepared in draft, copies were sent to the eighty institutions, requesting comment and criticism. No serious factual errors were thus disclosed. Suggestions concerning emphasis and interpretation were considered in writing the final draft.

A word remains to be said concerning the organization of the report. The next chapter summarizes the chief aspects of the tenure plans and practices found in the eighty institutions. This summary is intended to be a pre-

[12] The principal—but by no means only—difference between the institutions included and those excluded is that the tenure plans of the former are subject to the control of governing boards whereas the plans of the latter are often set forth in statutory enactments of legislatures.

7

liminary compendium for use by those interested either in revamping or establishing a tenure plan in a particular college or university; as far as we know, no such compilation is now available.[13] A few preliminary evaluations have been brought into this chapter, but every effort has been made to keep them recognizably distinguishable from the main body of the analytical statement. Chapter III deals with the legal problems presented by the plans and practices. The final chapter contains conclusions and recommendations.

[13] See Thomas I. Emerson and David Haber, *Political and Civil Rights in the United States* (1952), 880: "There is no current compilation of tenure rules and practices presently in force in American colleges and universities."

II

Plans and Practices

THE widely held belief that tenure is a major character-istic of higher education in the United States is supported by the fact that nearly all the eighty colleges and univer-sities included in this study confer some measure of tenure, either under a formal plan or by established practice. How-ever, the plans and practices indicate a bewildering assort-ment of criteria and procedures governing acquisition and termination of tenure. It is first necessary, therefore, to analyze and collate the criteria and procedures. Thereafter their legal significance will be considered.

ACQUISITION OF TENURE

Among the eighty colleges and universities, twenty-four institutions provide for automatic acquisition of tenure by a teacher, whatever his rank may be, after he has served a specified number of years. A larger group of forty-five institutions confer tenure when a teacher is appointed or promoted to a particular professorial rank, or after he has served a specified number of years at a particular professorial rank or combination of ranks. These two groups, which together total sixty-nine and make up 86 per cent of the total number studied, have set forth their standards for acquisition of tenure in plans which have been officially adopted by a board of trustees or other governing authority.

Eight of the colleges and universities confer tenure as a matter of practice, although in different degrees they fall short of official adoption of a specific tenure plan. Another institution, counted in the group of forty-five noted above, is also considered here because it confers tenure in practice upon instructors and assistant professors. Only three of the eighty institutions do not recognize tenure, and two of these are theological seminaries where the teachers have status as ordained ministers.[1]

In short, tenure is virtually universal among these eighty institutions, and the great majority have officially adopted plans which serve to guide the administration and the teachers. The real question, therefore, is the nature of the plans and practices—the standards and procedures which govern acquisition.

Automatic Acquisition of Tenure

The term "automatic acquisition of tenure" needs explanation, because the principle involved is often misunderstood, sometimes produces a hostile reaction, and is occasionally explicitly rejected.[2] What it means is that an in-

[1] Augustana Theological Seminary and Lutheran Theological Seminary at Gettysburg. For the third "no tenure" institution, Golden Gate College, see below, note 19.

[2] A frequently met provision that all appointments and promotions require specific action by the governing board is not regarded

dividual who has served an institution for a specified
length of time (and in some places also met a required test
of rank achievement) and who is continued in his post
acquires tenure. It is essential to note that there should be
nothing automatic about the evaluation by the institution
which leads to a decision to continue a teacher in its service; in this area the institution has full freedom of judgment. The criteria for automatic acquisition are therefore
nothing more than the rules by which an institution com-
mits itself to grant tenure to a teacher who is adjudged
competent and retained in employment after the probationary period.

Twenty-four of the institutions have "automatic acquisition" plans which govern all ranks; they confer tenure on
any teacher if he is reappointed after a specific number of
years.[3] The most frequently encountered term of years is

in this study as essential rejection of automatic acquisition. As an
example of explicit rejection, note the statement by the president
of a California college: "I personally, and the . . . Board of Trustees, have opposed the national policy of the A.A.U.P. that anyone who has taught for seven years shall enjoy tenure. It has
seemed to us that such an extension dilutes and eventually may
destroy the concept of tenure, which we regard as very important."
This institution gives tenure to the two top ranks after a term of
service at any rank, thus relating automatic acquisition to those
ranks; but it does not offer tenure to the person who could be retained beyond seven years at the two lower ranks.

See also below, note 9, on Wilson College.

[3] Academy of the New Church, Albright College, Blackburn
College, Bradley University, California Institute of Technology,
Carnegie Institute of Technology, Carthage College, College of Os-
teopathic Physicians and Surgeons, De Paul University, Elmhurst
College, Franklin and Marshall College, Garrett Biblical Institute,
Geneva College, Gettysburg College, Greenville College, Knox
College, McKendree College, Moravian College, Pennsylvania State
University, Swarthmore College, Thiel College, Wheaton College,

seven, resulting from agreement with or adoption of the standard recommended in the 1940 "Statement of Principles" of the American Association of University Professors and the Association of American Colleges.[4] The shortest period is one year, at Geneva College.[5] The longest is at the Carnegie Institute of Technology, fourteen years.[6]

Although the inquiry addressed to the eighty institutions did not specifically call for comment on the merits of "all-rank" automatic acquisition of tenure, it is interesting to find that, in response to the invitation to furnish general comment, only one institution offered adverse criticism of all-rank automatic acquisition. The absence of express opposition, coupled with present use of this system in 30 per cent of the institutions, suggests the possibility of ultimate widespread adoption of this kind of plan.

---

and two Pennsylvania colleges (restricted answers). The phrase "restricted answer," used here and in subsequent footnotes, indicates that the institution replying asked not to be identified; see the choice offered in the questionnaire, reproduced in Appendix B, p. 166 below. Service usually must be full-time and continuous except by special arrangement (as for off-campus research, government or military service, sabbatical leave, etc.). Service at special rank (as visiting professor, lecturer, etc.) appears not to count toward tenure.

[4] "Beginning with appointment to the rank of full-time instructor or a higher rank, the probationary period should not exceed seven years. . . ." See above, p. 1.

[5] Charter and bylaws in process of revision.

[6] This institution has a maximum progression system of three one-year terms as instructor, two three-year terms as assistant professor, and one five-year term as associate professor. A reliable unofficial opinion indicates that tenure is usually acquired in eight to eleven years; initial appointments are often made at the rank of assistant professor.

Forty-five institutions, more than half of those surveyed, confer tenure automatically upon achievement of a designated rank or by applying a standard which combines both period of service and rank. These forty-five constitute a "term-rank" group; since the full professorship is the highest ordinary rank, teachers at that level in all these places come under an automatic acquisition plan.[7] Associate professors are less generously included; assistant professors, much less; and instructors, not at all.

Full professors receive tenure immediately upon attaining their rank, whether by promotion or initial appointment, at fourteen institutions.[8] Sixteen plans give tenure

[7] A few of the all-rank institutions have particular provisions relating to tenure acquisition by full professors; such institutions could be included in the term-rank group here discussed; but since the emphasis of the study is on tenure acquisition rather than the prerogatives of a rank, these institutions have been placed in the all-rank group.

[8] Augustana College ("ordinarily"), California College of Arts and Crafts, Chicago Theological Seminary, Illinois Institute of Technology, Lutheran Theological Seminary at Philadelphia, Northwestern University, Pomona College ("ordinarily"), Scripps College, Seabury-Western Theological Seminary, Stanford University, University of California, University of Pennsylvania (probationary period possible but not usual), University of Southern California, and a Pennsylvania university (restricted answer). Stanford presents a paradox. The administration states that: "our long-standing practice is to appoint or promote to the rank of professor, without termination date, and to consider such appointment as automatically granting tenure." This statement has controlled Stanford's classification in this chapter. In contrast, faculty opinion at this institution states that the administrative officials and department heads are "acquainted with and fully respect the AAUP principles of tenure"; this, of course, would place Stanford in the all-rank automatic acquisition group. In further contrast, on the other side, the institution officially operates under a 1907 resolution of the trustees which merely sets forth periods of appointment.

13

immediately to the senior rank if it is achieved by promotion, but only after a probationary period if by initial appointment.[9] Thirteen institutions give tenure to full professors after a period of service including service at lower ranks.[10] Two colleges give tenure at this rank only after a period of service subsequent to promotion or appointment to the full professorship.[11]

The general picture for full professors in the term-rank

[9] Claremont Men's College, Dickinson College, Elizabethtown College, Haverford College, Lafayette College, La Salle College, Lincoln University, Mills College, Muhlenberg College, Rockford College, U.S. Naval Postgraduate School, University of Chicago, University of Illinois, University of Pittsburgh, Wilson College, and a Pennsylvania university (restricted answer). The probationary periods range from zero to five years, the chief cluster being three years; four institutions (Chicago, Dickinson, Haverford, and Illinois) do not name a specific period.

The bylaws of Wilson College state that "Professors upon first appointment shall be appointed for three years. If renewed, the appointment shall be for long term or without limit of term and shall be construed as establishing, in general, a reasonable expectation of permanency." A similar construction is stated for appointment to the top rank by promotion. However, the president states that "the Trustees have firmly set their faces against automaticity," and that the tenure provision "may be construed as automatic only if the Education Committee [of the Board] and the Board itself agree that promotion is desirable." Wilson College would be classified as lacking in automatic criteria except for the fact that all professors *do* appear to have tenure.

[10] The period ranges from two to ten years. Allegheny College, Bryn Mawr College, Illinois Wesleyan University, Immaculate Heart College, King's College, Millikin University, Occidental College, Roosevelt University, and Wilkes College consider service at any rank; Beaver College, Temple University, and Westminster College consider service at any professorial rank; Bucknell counts service only at the level of full or associate professor.

[11] Lake Forest College (3 years) and St. Vincent College (2 years).

group of forty-five institutions is thus one of rather even division among those who achieve tenure at once with their rank, those who must wait if initial appointment is to that rank, and those who must meet a general requirement as to length of staff service. The various plans are distributed without discernible pattern among large and small, new and old colleges and universities.

The situation with regard to associate professors is much like that of full professors except that only thirty-five institutions give tenure to associate professors when achievement of the rank, as well as term of service, is a consideration. Among the thirty-five, associate professors have tenure immediately, whether by promotion or initial appointment, at nine places; [12] immediately by promotion, but only after a probationary period if by appointment, at another eight places; [13] after a period of service including service at lower ranks in fifteen institutions; [14] and after

[12] Augustana College ("ordinarily"), California College of Arts and Crafts, Chicago Theological Seminary, Dickinson College, Scripps College, Seabury-Western Theological Seminary, University of California, University of Pennsylvania, and University of Southern California.

[13] Claremont Men's College, Illinois Institute of Technology, Lafayette College, Lincoln University, University of Chicago, University of Illinois, University of Pittsburgh, and a Pennsylvania university (restricted answer); the median is three years; the last three named do not specify the term.

[14] Allegheny College, Beaver College (service as associate or assistant professor only), Bryn Mawr College, Haverford College, Illinois Wesleyan University, Immaculate Heart College, Millikin University, Mills College, Muhlenberg College, Occidental College, Roosevelt University, Temple University, Westminster College, Wilkes College, and a Pennsylvania university (restricted answer). The probationary periods range from two to ten years; the approximate median is five years.

a period of service at that rank, however reached, at three places.[15]

The assistant professorship appears to be regarded everywhere as intrinsically a pretenure rank. None of the institutions gives tenure immediately upon achievement of that rank or after a probationary period if initially appointed to it. In twenty institutions assistant professors acquire tenure after a period of service, including service at a lower rank.[16]

Assistant professors, unlike their seniors, are in some institutions affected by an "up or out" policy. The University of Southern California has a five-year period at this rank, after which there is promotion with tenure to associate professor or termination of service. Lafayette College, the Illinois Institute of Technology, and the University of Chicago apply the same rules on a six-year basis. Northwestern University and the United States Naval Postgraduate School have "up or out" plans, but promotion does not necessarily give tenure.

Haverford College appears to be unique in having an age criterion for tenure at the level of assistant professor (and instructor):

Academic tenure may be accorded to a faculty member below the rank of associate professor who has served the college

[15] Bucknell University and Lake Forest College (4 years), and Northwestern University (5 years).

[16] Allegheny College, Beaver College, Bryn Mawr College, Bucknell University, Dickinson College, Haverford College, Illinois Institute of Technology, Lafayette College, Lincoln University, Millikin University, Muhlenberg College, Occidental College, Roosevelt University, Scripps College, Temple University, University of Chicago, University of Pittsburgh, University of Southern California, Westminster College, and Wilkes College.

for seven or more years. . . . In general it will be the policy of the college not to accord tenure to those in this group until they have attained the age of forty years.[17]

The instructorship is also regarded as a pretenure rank. The "up or out" principle affects instructors at eight places. The time range is from three to six years; the median is about five years; one institution states "several years." [18] Haverford College, as for assistant professors, has a minimum age of forty.

It is of course important to remember that an over-all view of the forty-five plans giving consideration to rank achievement must take into account the fact that twenty-four other plans have an automatic all-rank system based only on term of service. Schematically, the larger term-rank group of forty-five may be regarded as a kind of superstructure based upon the smaller all-rank group.

Tenure Granted in Practice without Official Commitment

Eight of the eighty colleges and universities confer tenure upon some faculty members although the board of trustees or other final institutional authority has not officially adopted a tenure plan. Another institution is considered in this section because, although it has officially adopted tenure for professors and associate professors, some of its assistant professors and instructors are given tenure

[17] "Haverford College: Statement on Academic Freedom and Tenure" (1950), p. 1.

[18] After three years: Northwestern University and University of Southern California. After four years: U.S. Naval Postgraduate School and University of Chicago. After six years: Illinois Institute of Technology, Roosevelt University, and a Pennsylvania university (restricted answer). After "several years": Lafayette College.

in practice but not under an official plan. These institutions are of particular interest, because study of their practices sheds historical light on the tenure-plan concept and reveals some of the uncertainties and tensions operating in this area. It is reasonable to assume that some of the institutions which now have plans passed through a phase of "practice without commitment" in their earlier history.[19]

The nine institutions are Chatham College, Crozer Theological Seminary, Drexel Institute of Technology, Illinois College, Lebanon Valley College, Loyola University of Los Angeles, MacMurray College, the University of California, and the University of Redlands. It is interesting to note the variety in size and nature of the colleges and universities which fall into a grouping because they grant tenure without official commitment. And since the picture is one of practice, the analysis will necessarily be somewhat more discursive than that of institutions with official plans.

Chatham College (chartered 1869) is a private, nondenominational college with fifty teachers. The college's "Statement on Tenure," adopted by the trustees in 1955, requires that a person holding an ordinary staff appointment at any of the professorial ranks "must be considered for Continuous Tenure" after a trial period, three years for

[19] Golden Gate College does not have tenure by explicit statement of its administration. The reply states: "We could answer some of the questions, of course, but the fact is we don't have any policy on 'tenure' . . . We have given some thought to tenure for our full-time teachers and have a faculty committee and a trustee committee working on it. . . . As a matter of record we have not discharged more than two teachers in the last 25 years, after two years of teaching. In both cases the cause would have resulted in dismissal in any college. . . ."

the two higher ranks and six years for assistant professors. There is no indication in the "Statement" of the status of teachers who are considered and then denied tenure. In reply to a query on this point, the president states:

This is not an "up or out" policy such as many institutions have. Any appointment after that point [of automatic consideration of tenure] is on a strictly annual basis. No limit has been set on the length of non-tenure service although our experience thus far indicates that such service does not ordinarily last over a period of more than three years or thereabouts.

The range of possible results under a principle of this kind is obviously unlimited, depending upon the interaction of institutional generosity and the market for teachers. Chatham has forty-two full-time teachers, of whom sixteen are on tenure appointment.

Crozer Theological Seminary (chartered 1867) [20] is a Baptist institution. The bylaws state that "all members of the faculty shall be elected by the Board of Trustees for a temporary period of three years, after which an indefinite tenure may be approved by the Board of Trustees upon recommendation of the President of the Seminary." Nothing is said about status after adverse decision.

Drexel Institute of Technology (chartered 1894) is a private, nondenominational institution, employing 253 teachers, 198 full time and 105 on tenure. A 1934 bylaw of the trustees provides:

b) All new appointees of rank higher than that of instructor will be employed by annual contract during the first three years of their service.

[20] Although the questionnaire was not answered, the charter and bylaws were furnished to the Project.

c) All faculty members of more than three years' service and of professorial rank may, upon recommendation of the Dean of their respective Schools, be employed on indefinite tenure, without necessity of annual contract.

The letter of notification sent to indefinite tenure appointees states merely that they shall hold office "during the pleasure of the Board." (The ambiguous character of this language is discussed in Chapter III, pages 88–90.)

Further light on the Drexel situation comes from that institution's reply to the questionnaire. It was stated that "current practice is described" in a quotation from the minutes of a faculty meeting of April 14, 1954:

[President] Creese spoke to the faculty in regard to tenure. Under the present plan any person who has been here for three years of full-time employment and has attained the rank of assistant professor, would come up for definite tenure. The new plan provides that an appointee would normally receive one-year contracts for a period of three years, then a two-year contract, and thereafter would be considered for appointment on indefinite tenure if he had also attained the rank of assistant professor.

Thus, the 1934 rule of the trustees providing for tenure after three years for the rank of assistant professor or higher has been modified—not by trustee action, but by administrative practice—to a five-year rule. Presumably the trustees approve of the change. Under either rule, old or new, the probationary term leads only to tenure eligibility and not to acquisition by any automatic criterion.

Illinois College (chartered 1835) is a private, nondenominational (but Christian-oriented) college. The administration states that there is neither official nor unofficial definition of tenure and that there is no automatic acquisition in practice. The bylaws of the trustees provide:

The initial appointment of Professors shall be for one year, after which term they may be given permanent appointments of indefinite term, it being understood that the term of appointment may be terminated by either party to the contract upon reasonable notice. . . . Associate Professors—The initial appointment of Associate Professors shall be for one year. They may thereafter be appointed for terms of three years, with permanent tenure possible after one three-year term. . . . Assistant Professors—The initial appointment of Assistant Professors shall be for one year. They may thereafter be appointed for terms of two years. . . . Instructors—[annual appointment].

The purely permissive nature of accordance of tenure (to professors and associate professors) cannot be said to indicate a tenure system; however, it should be noted that 60 per cent of the full-time staff (fifteen out of twenty-five) are stated to have tenure. Responsible faculty opinion recognizes that the phrase "reasonable notice" "could mean no real tenure at all." This same opinion "can find no unfairness through the past twenty-five years"—except on the part of one or two teachers who left without giving adequate notice. Illinois College thus presents a picture of apparently good practice inadequately supported by official commitment.

Lebanon Valley College (chartered 1867) is an institution of the Evangelical United Brethren Church with a denominationally selected board. A rather detailed statement on "Academic Rank, Promotion and Tenure" was adopted in 1956.[21] On tenure, the statement says:

[21] A "Statement of Policy Concerning Academic Rank, Promotion and Tenure" was adopted in 1956; it refers to a five-year probationary period, but tenure is not clearly automatically acquired at its conclusion.

The first five years of initial employment shall be a probationary period. . . .

Tenure at Lebanon Valley College provides for a continuing series of term appointments which may be terminated by the college only for cause. . . .

After a teacher has completed his probationary period and has been found worthy of retention on the faculty and has been given tenure by the Board of Trustees, he will be notified by the president that he has achieved such status.

The implication of these passages is that tenure is acquired after five years, but the language is something less than conclusive. The finding that a teacher is "worthy of retention" and the granting of tenure by the board are not necessarily derivative from continued employment after completion of the probationary period. The institution reported that nineteen of the forty-six full-time staff members have tenure.

Loyola University of Los Angeles (chartered 1918) is controlled by the Society of Jesus; the trustees are members of that order; the regents are laymen who serve as advisors; and the final authority is the president. There are 101 teachers, 80 full-time, and 35 on tenure.

The president states: "Until the present, tenure has been associated with rank, but it is now our plan to bring the policy on tenure into closer agreement with the AAUP policy. Our policy when adopted will be incorporated in the Statutes of the University." [22] The policy to be established is an all-rank automatic acquisition system with a probationary period of seven years. It is of considerable interest that an institution under the complete control of a

[22] Only the "when adopted" condition stands in the way of placing Loyola in the all-rank automatic acquisition group.

religious society its about to give formal approval to the approved tenure-acquisition standards of the profession.[23]

MacMurray College (founded 1846, chartered 1863) is a private, Methodist-related college. Its 1953 statement on "Academic Freedom and Tenure" provides that "at the expiration of this [first, one-year] contract a new one may be made from year to year until the end of the fourth probationary year. Thereafter permanent tenure may be given the appointee." The president states that tenure is "never automatic," but it should be noted that thirty of the forty full-time teachers were stated to have tenure.

University of California (chartered 1868) has approximately 5,050 teachers, about 3,400 full-time and about 1,650 on tenure on its campuses. In response to the project questionnaire, this institution furnished a number of relevant documents; supplementary material was obtained, particularly the May 31, 1955, report of the Special Committee on Tenure of the Academic Senate (submitted with petition to the Board of Regents in 1956 and acted upon by that body in 1958).

Acquisition of tenure at the largest state university in the United States, at least with regard to automatic acquisition, can probably best be studied by examining the several positions taken at different times by the Regents and the Academic Senate. In 1920 the Regents officially adopted the principle "that appointment as associate or full professor carries with it security of tenure in the full academic

---

[23] The dean of another Jesuit institution (where professors and associate professors acquire tenure) makes an interesting comment: "I feel that tenure in a Jesuit institution does not have the importance in the eyes of the lay faculty that it has in lay-controlled institutions. The controlling group in a Jesuit institution is a dedicated body of men, who foster a family spirit in the faculty."

sense." In 1939 the Academic Senate recommended tenure for professors and associate professors, an "up or out" rule for assistant professors at the end of a second three-year term, and an "up or out" rule for instructors at the end of five years. Retention at the slowest rate of promotion could therefore have yielded tenure at the end of eleven years. In 1947 the Senate proposed that the assistant professor's term of service be changed to three two-year appointments; for instructors it was stated that "service in this rank should not exceed two years." The probationary terms for the two lower ranks were brought together in the recommendation of an "eight-year rule":

Officers of instruction who have served for terms in excess of a total of eight years in the grades of assistant professor and instructor [and lecturers and associates on more than half-time] . . . or in any sequence of these grades, should thereby have achieved tenure by reason of length of service.

In 1947, as before, it was recommended that the two upper ranks carry tenure.

The University of California administration publishes the *Orientation Handbook for Faculty Members,* which in the 1954 edition states:

The Resolutions of the Academic Senate as to Appointments, Promotions and Tenure, while not adopted by the Regents, have been accepted by the President as a guide.

[With respect to professors and associate professors, the By-laws of the Regents are noted to the effect that] . . . appointment and promotion of faculty members . . . shall be voted by the Board on the recommendation of the President."

The *Orientation Handbook* quotes the six-year and two-year "up or out" provisions of the Senate Manual for assistant professors and instructors; nothing is said about the "eight-year" rule.

In 1956 the faculty completed adoption of a committee report which again recommends tenure for the upper ranks and the eight-year rule for the lower ranks. In the accompanying petition which transmitted this report to the Regents, official provision of tenure is asked for the upper ranks, but for the lower ranks, in place of the eight-year rule, the Regents were asked to rule that assistant professors and instructors could acquire "continuous tenure by reason of length of service."

Finally, on December 19, 1958 (as these pages were being set in type), the Regents adopted a resolution stating:

All appointments to the position of Professor and Associate Professor and to positions of equivalent rank (see Section 2 (a) of Chapter VI) are continuous in tenure until terminated by retirement, demotion or dismissal. Appointments to academic positions below the rank of Associate Professor may acquire tenure by reason of length of service under rules prescribed by the President and with the approval of the Board.

Consequently, it is now possible that the president will prescribe and the Regents approve a tenure rule for the lower ranks, and this rule may embody a specified probationary period. If these developments take place, California will join the group of twenty-four institutions which grant tenure automatically at all ranks after a term of service.[24]

[24] The coincidence of the December 19, 1958, regental action with the beginning of manufacture of this book permits only brief notice and tentative opinion on this latest phase of the University of California tenure system. Readers with a particular interest in that institution should seek information about likely further developments.

In recent years the question of tenure at California has of course been intermingled with the loyalty oath dispute.[25] On March 30, 1956, the Regents granted back pay (and pension and sabbatical rights) to sixteen dismissed teachers with tenure who were restored to their posts by the state supreme court.

University of Redlands (chartered 1907) is a private, Baptist-related university with a large majority of the trustees chosen denominationally. There are 103 teachers, 81 full-time and 28 on tenure.

The question of automatic criteria at Redlands can best be considered by examining a trustees' bylaw, the informal "Recommendations to the Faculty" (a statement adopted by the faculty), and the president's explanations of current practice. These three statements are markedly different in nature. The bylaw provides:

Terms of Appointments. (1) Appointments to the Faculty shall be of two kinds, temporary and permanent. . . . A temporary appointment is one which [is] terminated at the close of the period for which the appointment is made. A permanent appointment shall continue during the life of the teacher. . . . (2) All first appointments . . . shall be temporary and for a period of one or two years, except that an appointment to a full professorship may be for five years or on permanent tenure. (3) All appointments to the rank of Instructor shall be temporary, and for not over two years. (4) Appointments to the rank of Assistant Professor, subsequent to the initial appointment, shall be for three or five years. (5) Appointments to the rank of Associate Professor, subsequent to the period of initial appointment, shall be for five years.

[25] See George R. Stewart, *The Year of the Oath* (1950); and *AAUP Bulletin* 42: 64–66 (1956); 44: 503 (1958).

(6) Appointment to the rank of Professor, subsequent to the period of initial appointment, shall be for not less than five years nor more than eight.

. . . In the event that a teacher on permanent appointment fails, or is unable to maintain his full professional efficiency, he may be transferred to a lower rank with less exacting duties.

The approach of the teaching staff to the question of tenure is embodied in a faculty committee report, "Recommendations to the Faculty," adopted by the faculty in 1947. The president characterizes this report as "a semiofficial statement used as a guide line, but not as a law or official document to be followed to the letter. . . . [It] has been reviewed periodically and is basic when considering promotion and salary increments." "Recommendations to the Faculty" sets up tenure criteria distinctly different from those of the trustees' bylaw; it advises that "on the basis of these recommended [promotion] standards, permanent tenure be granted to professors and associate professors at the end of the third year, and to assistant professors and instructors not later than at the end of six years."

Finally, in reply to the questionnaire sent out in connection with this study, the president comments on present practice:

While we have not changed the By-laws we are operating slightly differently in recent years concerning appointments of faculty members. We are trying to comply with the recommendations of the committee on academic tenure of the Association of American University Professors and arrange appointments so that individuals who have served on the University faculty for a period of six years may be those who are capable of being appointed on tenure. This means that we do not strictly adhere to the policy of granting tenure with a third contract. Under no condition do we consider tenure automatic and tenure is given a faculty member only when a faculty member has been specifically voted on tenure by . . . the Board.

Tenure at Redlands, under the bylaws, is stated to be permanent for some teachers, but it is in fact subordinated to term appointments, and acquisition is unimplemented by automatic criteria. The faculty has recommended a plan which conforms in general to the norm of the profession. The administration appears to be attempting a practice which will not contradict either the rule of the governing board or the standards of the faculty. It is problematical whether, in a crisis situation, such divergent positions could continue to exist without open conflict.

Evaluative Criteria for Acquisition of Tenure

Judgment on a teacher's competence, promise, and usefulness precedes, and is the basis of, an institution's decision to retain him in employment or to place him at a particular rank—and thereby to give him tenure. Such a judgment involves the evaluative criteria for acquisition of tenure. The nature of these criteria, and the extent to which they are "available" by being made known to faculties, are clearly aspects of the tenure plan, even though they are not always incorporated in the formal statement of that plan.

With regard to availability, half of the eighty colleges and universities here surveyed indicated their evaluative criteria in their replies to the questionnaire. In several instances, however, the criteria described do not appear to be embodied in any document routinely made available to the teaching staff; and, in most instances where a description is offered, the criteria are not specifically related to tenure acquisition. These defects in communication and clearly defined applicability are probably not overwhelmingly serious, for most of the institutions somewhere in their publications say something about the qualities they regard important for initial appointment or promotion. The teacher whose interest is in tenure can reasonably infer a good deal.

As for the nature of the standards, a bringing-together of all the qualities deemed desirable in all these institutions produces something like an index to the aspirations of American higher education: advanced degrees; teaching experience and teaching power; proved research capacity; publications; attendance at and participation in professional society meetings; committee work and other kinds of intramural faculty service; effective personal relations with students and in student guidance; compatibility with the campus community; service to the local general community and to the nation; and national reputation.

Classification of these evaluative criteria would probably not be a very useful exercise, because it would yield mainly groupings of words. Such terms as "teaching power," "research capacity," and "intramural faculty service" have meaning only in particular situations. When the particular situation is a decision on tenure, a complex of facts and value systems becomes relevant: the traditions and standards of the institution, the experience and wisdom of the judges, and the merits of the person being judged. The result is hardly something to be measured. This is as it should be in the delicate operation of assessing a professional person.

Nevertheless, publication by an institution of its evaluative criteria can be genuinely useful. In a specific milieu, where words and actions have a common significance, announced standards provide a framework for such important operations as the granting of tenure. Even though the meaning and force of the criteria is localized, their development should be sought by all concerned—trustees, administrators, and faculty.

Stanford University offers a sound approach through its "guidance sheet" given to the Advisory Board subcommittee which is charged with personnel action. Forty questions are asked, and it is clear that adequate answers will not only cover in detail the candidate's merits but also require thoughtful self-scrutiny by those who are doing the judging. The following are illustrative questions concerning the candidate:

Will his duties impinge on those of any other member of the staff? If so, are the relations likely to be cordial?

Does he observe an appropriate relationship between his specialty and larger intellectual or social problems? Does he have a tendency to allow competing interests to distract from his principal professional specialty?

What is the strongest evidence of exceptional intellectual ability?

The responsibility of those engaged in personnel decisions is emphasized by such questions as:

How extensive was the search for a candidate?

Will his duties impinge on the activities of any other department? If so, has there been consultation with the other department?

If he has not taught at Stanford, did you seek evaluation of the candidate by those who know his professional work?

If the candidate is Stanford trained, what consideration has been given the matter of in-breeding?

An important question for many teachers is that of a quantitative distribution of their energy between "research" and "teaching." Recognizing that in a perfect educational world there should be no conflict between the two activities —and that in fact they become one at the highest level of performance—teachers sense that different institutions will make widely different demands. At some major institutions, teachers will understand that research activity is a prime requirement; the allocation of energy will be a relatively simple matter. But at a smaller college, or within the liberal arts college of some universities, uncertainty about emphasis can exist and cause frustration or even failure. In the latter instance, a forthright statement by the institution can be very helpful. An excellent example is the statement by Claremont College:

In a small, high-tuition college like Claremont Men's College, more emphasis should be placed upon teaching ability and less upon research than is the practice in large universities. It might be reasonable to say that, whereas the emphasis is 3/4 upon research and 1/4 upon teaching in many large universities, these emphases should be reversed in Claremont.

It is clear, however, that to maintain the type of teaching which Claremont Men's College desires, some research activity is necessary. Research activity is defined as including writing for publication, lecturing, or public or professional service. Lack of any research output would normally be considered a complete bar to full professorial appointment and a substantial bar to associate professorial appointment except as noted below. Failure to complete the doctor's degree should normally be a bar to associate professor appointment.

Persons teaching repetitive, drill type, under-graduate courses, such as mathematics, statistics, or English composition, may be promoted on the basis of superior teaching performance. Promotion to the rank of associate professor would normally be somewhat slower, however, than for persons who have made research contributions. Promotion to full professorship would be even longer delayed. Moreover, such persons should carry a larger teaching load than those from whom research contributions are expected.

Persons who hold important administrative assignments and are part-time teachers may be promoted to associate professorships without research output, but only after a longer period of time than is required for those persons with research output. Normally, however, such non-research persons will not receive full professorial appointments except as a token of esteem a short time before retirement.

Another kind of problem sometimes arises from a religious commitment by a college or university, which may produce a later misunderstanding between the institution and an individual teacher. For example, both parties may happily have agreed to the filling of a teaching post in mathematics, and nothing much may have been said about anything except professional considerations; later, to the discomfort of all, the teacher discovers that the institution has a firm doctrinal commitment, and the college finds that it has on its hands an unmistakable religious indifferentist. Even if such divergence is jointly ignored or tolerated, it may adversely affect tenure acquisition. The answer, surely, is candor, on both sides. As to the institution, one welcomes the frankness of a statement like that of Greenville College, where teachers are told that they are expected to "be in full sympathy with the standards of conduct and Biblical doctrine held by Greenville College and interpreted by the

Methodist Church, . . . [to] have a positive testimony of a personal Christian experience, . . . [and desirably to] have demonstrated . . . wholesome spiritual influence and leadership."

Still another general standard is "co-operation." Every working community attempts to cultivate a co-operative spirit among its members; failure to work together may, as will be seen later in the discussion of grounds for dismissal, even lead to tenure termination. Admittedly, the growth of such a spirit depends upon the successful working out of each year's myriad of human relationships, but a forthright statement of the goal sought can at least offer guidance. The standard announced by the Chicago Theological Seminary —a standard broadly enough conceived to be useful to any institution—is unusually explicit:

In addition to teaching capacity, productive capacity, promise of continuing growth, "character," we consider important a man's capacity to engage in what we call "conversation" with his colleagues on the faculty. A man with a dogmatic attitude of mind, unwilling or unable to learn from others or to engage in intellectual give-and-take, unwilling to add to the cooperative thinking of the faculty, is not a candidate for tenure.

Finally, some notice should be taken of the "psychology" which surrounds the application of evaluative criteria. First appointment to a post ordinarily means that a teacher with acceptable training and skills has received a preliminary favorable judgment. It should mean, for him, that in the next few years he will be able to put his mind on his work without too much worry about his personal future. But the teacher also senses the reality of the situation; he knows that his senior colleagues and the administration are

33

engaged in a series of cumulative assessments which will eventually come to a focus in a decision on tenure. Where, the teacher may ask, should the balance lie? Should he think only of doing the best job he can, or should he sometimes give some regard to the immediacies of his essentially competitive position? Certainly there is no simple answer. However, an institution may be well advised, in its own interests as well as those of its individual faculty members, to give such helpful assurances as it can.[26]

Governing Procedures

So far attention has been centered on the substantive elements in acquisition of tenure—length of service, rank, and evaluative criteria. It is now in order to examine the procedures by which standards are applied.

Human intangibles are of course an ever-present influence in procedures which govern personnel decisions. First, all the judgments—up and down the line—are made by individuals of differing personal authority and influence. A dean who commands less than the full respect of his faculty may, despite his official power of review, have a weaker voice in judgments on tenure than a distinguished professor who is merely "consulted." Second, these procedures are affected by the internal patterns of agreement and conflict which exist in all groups. For example, a de-

[26] Roosevelt University has a rule which establishes presumption of effectiveness: "Indefinite tenure is understood to be contingent upon adequate and efficient performance of duties assigned to the teacher, such duties to be those customarily regarded as academic. The burden of proof of inefficiency is to be on the administration and the Department Chairman if the teacher is not a Department Chairman; otherwise, the burden of proof is to be on the administration only."

34

partmental tradition of dedication to scholarship may cause the judgment of the staff to be quite the most significant part of the procedure. Contrariwise, a department torn by "politics" may produce judgments which a higher reviewing authority will feel bound to correct. Nevertheless, while intangible personal social elements are bound to play their part, stated procedures have the considerable merit of an announced norm. They at least offer a known pattern for doing business, and marked departures from that pattern will need explanation.

The chief kinds of action in procedure for acquisition of tenure are initiation of the recommendation, consultation, and review (which at the final stage officially grants or denies tenure). An over-all view of the procedures indicates a loose pattern of progression from initiation of the tenure recommendation up through channels of consultation and review. In its simplest form this progression is from staff to dean, to president, to governing board— sometimes with participation by a general faculty committee or faculty-administration committee at an intermediate point. If the recommendation is initiated in some middle phase, as by a dean, there is often consultation of the lower echelons. But one must constantly be on the lookout for reverse currents, parallel and mixed actions, and so forth, all in bewildering variety.

Before turning to the procedures themselves, it will be helpful to note briefly the make-up and functions of the groups involved, and the authority assigned to the chief administrative officials.

The departmental teaching staff. Action on a tenure recommendation is understandably often limited to part of the staff: persons holding rank higher than that of the

35

candidate, the members with tenure, the professorial group, the full professors, or the voting members.

The department head. Many American colleges and universities give particular responsibility and authority to a department head. Sometimes he is specifically charged with initiating tenure recommendations. Action of this kind, for the purposes of this study, can be regarded as essentially administrative because the head functions as the first link in a chain of administrative authority. Obviously, by his position, he is also in an important degree responsible for his teaching colleagues and therefore a spokesman for their faculty point of view.

The general faculty committee. All-college or all-university committees are often met. Some of these committees are charged with all matters relating to faculty appointment, promotion, and welfare; some are committees on appointment and promotion; others concern themselves only with tenure (occasionally coupled with academic freedom). These groups are usually appointed by the administration, although some are nominated and elected by the faculty.

The dean (or deans). The extraordinary range of authority in the American college deanship is a commonplace; quite apart from variations dependent on personality, there are deans who in matters of tenure are merely advisers to the president, and others who have almost final responsibility for academic judgment. In the larger institutions procedure often calls for action by both the college or school dean and by a dean of faculties, a provost, or a vice-president for educational administration.

The faculty-administration committee. Some institutions have mixed groups at work in this matter; the faculty element is variously faculty-elected, administration-appointed, or ex officio.

The president. It is beyond the scope of this study to discuss the unique position of the American college or university president. But in general terms it may fairly be said that his multiple responsibilities—many of which he alone must carry—have necessarily brought him an extraordinary degree of power. However, with regard to decisions on tenure, the president's authority is perhaps most wisely exercised in terms of over-all judgment, leaving to the teaching staff the main responsibility of individual decisions.[27]

The governing board. The governing board of a college or university nearly always bears the ultimate legal responsibility for the contractual obligations of the institution, including the employment of the teaching staff. Consequently, the official granting of tenure is the board's business. Sometimes the board acts directly as a whole, sometimes it reviews the action of one of its committees, sometimes it delegates final authority to a committee. In a few of the denominational institutions the action of the board is reviewed by a superior church body, or, rarely, the board is subordinate to the president.

The existence of so many groups and persons likely to have responsibility for decisions on acquisition of tenure naturally raises the question whether one may not expect

[27] Recognizedly, the president will have to exercise extraordinary authority when he faces the problem of rehabilitating a "bankrupt" department.

The historical origins of the American college presidency should be borne in mind. See Richard Hofstadter and Walter P. Metzger, *The Development of Academic Freedom in the United States* (1955); particularly Pt. I, "The Age of the College."

as many kinds of procedures as there are institutions. Perhaps so, if each description were necessarily complete in all details. But among the eighty institutions studied, four main groupings may be discerned:

20 offer no statement about procedure;
25 reserve action to the administration;
10 reserve action to the administration but provide for faculty consultation; and
26 provide for some kind of faculty action other than mere consultation.

Twenty-five institutions reserve action to the administration; that is, decisions on acquisition of tenure are the business of the department head, the dean, the president, or the governing board, in a variety of combinations. At eleven colleges or universities the department head initiates the recommendation, at four the department head or dean, at three the president or the dean, at one a tripartite committee made up of department head, dean, and president, and at six the president.

Similar variety of procedure is found among the ten institutions which keep action in administrative hands but provide for faculty consultation. In five places the department head initiates the recommendation, and in five the president; in all these institutions either the departmental staff or the general faculty committee is consulted.[28] At

[28] At a major state university the president initiates, consulting the general faculty committee. The size of the staff and the known practice of this institution require the inference that presidential initiation of a tenure recommendation is in fact based upon a preceding (but unofficial) faculty judgment. There are probably other procedural systems where the explicit rule differs significantly from actual practice.

two among this group of ten, the candidate himself is officially "consulted," in one instance by a head-dean-president committee and in the other by the governing board—at its option.

The last group of twenty-six provides for faculty action at some point. The faculty action may be recognizably distinct, as in the judgments of a departmental staff or of an elected faculty committee; or it may be intermingled with administrative action, as in the work of a faculty-administration committee; or it may possibly be tinged by an administrative point of view, as in the case of an administration-appointed faculty committee. The recommendation for tenure is initiated by the departmental staff at seven institutions,[29] by a general faculty committee at another seven,[30] and by a faculty-administration committee at two. Faculty review of recommendations made by the administration, as distinguished from initiation action, is provided for at ten institutions. Six provide for review by a general faculty committee,[31] and one calls for review by two different faculty-administration committees. No college or university has formally established review by the departmental staff.

Among this group of twenty-six, three institutions have practices which call for special comment. Two are Pennsylvania colleges where the procedure is based upon the Friends' concept of "consensus." In these colleges, in all matters relating to reappointment, all the members of the department involved (or sometimes only its senior mem-

[29] At three of these places the general faculty committee, the head, or any of the administrative officials may also initiate.

[30] At two of these places the administrative officials may also initiate.

[31] At one of these, "together" with the president.

bers), all the administrators, the chairman of the general
faculty committee (and some of its members), all discuss
a candidacy with each other. The result is described by an
administrative correspondent at one of these institutions:

In most cases there is considerable agreement. In some cases
there is sharp disagreement, which then requires continuing
review, discussion, and occasionally the consulting of faculty
members from other institutions who are thought to know
the candidate's work. In theory it would be possible for the
President and the . . . [general faculty committee] to come
to different decisions on a candidate but this has not happened in . . . (13 years).

The President recommends to the Board . . . with the
concurrence of the . . . [general faculty committee]. The
Board has final authority, specifically stated, but since 1917
when the Plan of Faculty Government was introduced the
Board has as far as . . . [the writer knows] always accepted
the recommendations made by the President with the concurrence of the . . . [general faculty committee].

At the second of these Quaker-tradition colleges, action on
tenure recommendation is by a committee of the three chief
administrative officers and the two faculty members of the
governing board.[32]

The other special comment relates to an institution already placed in the group where initiation and matters of
review are purely administrative procedure. It reappears in
this "faculty action" group because it offers an alternative
procedure whereby a teacher may himself initiate consideration of his promotion. He must first put his request to
his department head who is obliged to send his approval or

[32] See Charles P. Dennison, *Faculty Rights and Obligations*
(1955), comment on Haverford College.

disapproval to the dean; failing favorable action, the teacher may address the president (the head and dean being informed); still failing approval, the teacher may appeal to an appointed personnel committee of the faculty, and that group can either dismiss the case finally or send it on to the board for final adjudication.

Although caution must be exercised in appraising these procedures, two significant facts deserve emphasis. First, one-fourth of these eighty institutions offered no statement at all about procedure for acquisition of tenure. This deficiency, disturbing in itself, may also permit or even require inferences about the value of the substantive criteria at those places. Second, two-thirds of the colleges and universities in this cross section of American higher education have not provided for formal action by their faculties on questions of tenure acquisition. The absence of such action has two harmful results. It denies to these institutions the benefit of a formal expression of opinion by those who are best qualified to express a judgment. Further, it denies to the teachers judgment by their peers. Some palliation can be found in the consultative provisions, in the permissible assumption that even uncrystallized faculty opinion has a good deal of weight, and in the undoubted good will and good sense of many administrations. But, on the record, the judgment of the practicing profession on a mainly professional matter is not asked for in fifty-four out of eighty institutions.

Appeal from Denial of Tenure

A teacher who takes his doctor's degree at thirty, serves six or seven years in full harness, and then finds himself denied tenure—and probably not retained—confronts a grave crisis in his career. He is too old to compete on salary terms with new, less expensive Ph.D.'s, and his failure to achieve tenure is difficult to explain when he seeks a job elsewhere.

Some individuals in this situation will have to ask themselves whether they chose the right profession for the use of their talents. Not a few will be forced to recognize that, under competitive conditions, they have not shown the needed intellectual, scholarly, or pedagogic capacity. Some may discover themselves simply the victims of the financial inability of the institution they serve to award tenure status to all who deserve it.[33]

But from time to time there will be other teachers who consider themselves professionally qualified for appointment on tenure to vacancies which do exist and believe that they have not been correctly or fairly judged. For such persons, right or wrong as they may be in their individual opinions, it is highly desirable that there exist a stated right to appeal from denial of tenure, with appropriate procedure for the exercise of that right.

Thirty-five of the eighty institutions both recognize the right to appeal from denial of tenure and describe some kind of available procedure. Unfortunately, only in a few instances does the "faculty manual" or other similar document set forth the procedure; this is a deficiency in a needed emphasis, and in a particular case might operate materially to the disadvantage of a teacher. On the other hand, some of the institutions which have not adequately published this procedure do make known the general procedures that govern appeal from any kind of administrative decision.

[33] See Bernard N. Schilling, "De Rerum Natura: Supplement to Report of the Committee," *AAUP Bulletin* 42: 445–463 (1956).

Finally, although it is not always stated that the governing board ultimately reviews formal appeals from denial of tenure, it may be assumed that matters of this kind—because of their serious nature—would normally receive at least informal board consideration.

The teacher who seeks to initiate an appeal from denial of tenure may do so at various administrative levels in seventeen institutions; in six of these places he may appeal to the governing board. In thirteen colleges and universities he may lodge his appeal with the general faculty committee.[34] At five institutions the appeal is made to a faculty-administration committee.[35]

Thus in this important matter of seeking review of an adverse decision on tenure acquisition something less than half of the eighty institutions offer an avenue, and only thirteen or one-sixth of the whole group provide for a faculty judgment.

TERMINATION OF TENURE

A teacher dismissed from a tenure post faces the probable ending of his professional career. If the "cause" of his dismissal is his own serious lapse from professional integrity or morality, there is of course only the private matter of personal readjustment. If, however, the dismissal is improper or unjust, a problem arises—of concern to the whole profession—because an innocent teacher may not find him-

[34] One of these thirteen also permits initiation with the departmental staff. At another, review of denial must be initiated *by* the staff.

[35] At one major institution the teacher may raise appropriate questions when he believes his nonreappointment violates academic freedom or other similar policy, but may not raise the question of his competency.

self in a much better position than that of a wrongdoer. The public is not educated to make distinctions in these matters and tends to look to the result. Employment of a victim at another institution is unlikely; the administration and governing board would have to make an independent investigation of the merits of the case and, if their judgment was favorable, would perhaps have to defend their decision. Fellow teachers would be more intelligently curious but, even if they were determined to come to the rescue, might lack the power to help a man. In short, except where widespread public opinion recognizes that notorious injustice has been done, the dismissed teacher probably must start a new life.

A penalty of this magnitude should be imposed only upon significant and completely relevant grounds and under scrupulously fair procedures. The plans and practices relating to dismissal, with respect both to standards and procedures, unfortunately do not present a good picture. The criteria for dismissal are too often unnecessarily vague, and procedures often are deficient or nonexistent.

Criteria for Termination

A general view of all the criteria named by the eighty institutions here studied suggests that most of the colleges and universities have begun with the basic concept of "cause." This ground is sometimes set forth in that section of their charters which asserts the ultimate power of the trustees to discharge members of the staff. Later, in tenure plans and elsewhere, more specific grounds are added, such as incompetence and immorality.[36] Some places have a

[36] Interestingly, one institution has recently eliminated such specific grounds as incompetence and immorality, and returned to

standard of institutional loyalty. Church-related institutions usually bring in religious criteria.

The criteria for termination of tenure fall into a number of major groupings:

Cause. Eight institutions merely state "cause" without supplementary specific grounds. In these places, as well as in others where additional grounds are stated, "cause" is frequently qualified by "good," "adequate," "grave," "just," "justifiable," or "sufficient." These adjectives appear to be intended as a barrier against termination action based on trivial or inadequate grounds.

Professional incompetence. Forty-four colleges and universities state grounds which in one way or another constitute professional incompetence. Thirty use the word "incompetence" itself; others refer to "ineffective teaching," failure to give "satisfactory service," and "serious shortcomings in meeting duties." Ten institutions refer to "inefficiency."

Twenty-one plans ring the changes on "duty." "Neglect of duty" can of course be read without condemnatory connotation; but it is a fact that "neglect" occurs in a number of common phrases where it at least faintly suggests an element of moral weakness—as in "neglect of family." On the other hand, "inadequate performance of duty" appears to avoid subjective tonality and simply describes the situation as observed. These colorations also in some degree affect the word "duty" itself; in one context it may suggest ethical responsibility and in another no more than fulfillment of assigned responsibilities of a specifically academic nature.

"cause." See also below, p. 47, for discussion of the AAUP general ground of "adequate cause" and the collateral grounds of incompetence and moral turpitude.

Three institutions indicate that failure in professional growth can be a cause for termination. "Prolonged lack of productivity," "failure to advance professionally," and, most specifically, "failure to meet qualifications for advancement" are the terms used.

Immorality. Almost the same number of institutions, forty-five in all, say that immorality is a ground for termination of tenure. The term is "immorality" or "moral turpitude" in thirty-six instances; variations include infraction of "commonly accepted standards," "sexual immorality," and "drunkenness." "Misconduct," found in ten institutions, could perhaps be regarded as a general term roughly equivalent to "cause," but the context in which it appears usually indicates rather clearly that misconduct refers to personal immorality. Here also one meets frequent qualification; the misconduct is referred to as "grave," "gross," "proved gross," and "scandalous." The language perhaps becomes too broad in such criteria as "unbecoming conduct" and "unbecoming behavior."

Crime, including treason. Only six institutions name crime as a ground. If speculation is in order, this infrequency may be regarded as reflecting a view that immorality is a sufficiently inclusive term to cover criminal offense; or perhaps it is felt that the designation of criminal conduct may make more difficult termination of tenure because of immoral—though not criminal—behavior.

Twelve of the colleges and universities include treason or other political disloyalty as a ground. One refers to conduct defined as subversive by the Pennsylvania Loyalty Act; one refers to "failure to uphold the Constitution of the United States." One states the legally dubious ground of "advocating viewpoints which have been declared by a

competent court to be treasonable to the United States."
Treason, of course, is defined by the Constitution essentially in terms of overt acts; "viewpoints" are not even
unlawful, much less treasonable.

Incapacity or disability. Physical (and sometimes mental) incapacity or disability is named as a ground for termination in only nine institutions. Possibly some places
regard this ground as a suborder of incompetence and therefore avoid specific designation. But in the light of the
contexts of "incompetence"—and its cousins "inefficiency"
and "neglect of duty"—it appears desirable that there be
a ground of morally neutral implication, suggesting only the
medical accidents of life.

Grounds in the 1940 "Statement." Eight colleges and
universities indicate that the grounds for dismissal are those
set forth in the 1940 "Statement of Principles" adopted by
the American Association of University Professors and
the Association of American Colleges. That statement refers to "adequate cause" as the ground for termination, but
in other sections there are collateral references to "incompetence" and "moral turpitude." [37]

Failure in institutional relationship. Nine institutions state
that tenure can be terminated because of a failure by the
teacher in his relationship to his college or university. Four
refer to "disloyalty to policies and principles," or "lack of
co-operation with policies," or "lack of sympathy with
the founding purposes." Two specify "insubordination."
One institution has as a ground "bringing the good name
of the institution or its officers into public disrepute," and
another has "participation in such activities as might bring

[37] These eight institutions have also been counted in the groups
which give as grounds incompetence and moral turpitude.

47

discredit to the college." [38] Six of these nine institutions are denominational or church-related and for these six this class of grounds probably indicates a special concern about a particular institutional function.

But whatever the explanation may be, this standard is inherently dangerous to a firm concept of tenure. The language chosen is so broad, and so capable of being given almost any meaning, as to constitute, essentially, an "escape clause." And, at least for the religious institutions, it is not necessary because other more exact statements accomplishing the same end are ordinarily also to be found.

Religious criteria. Colleges or universities which have a religious base usually state some criterion embracing religious doctrine or practice; failure to observe this will lead to dismissal. Greenville College refers to "conduct or teaching contrary to the published standards of the institution which are furnished to candidates for election to the staff and are printed in the annual catalogue." St. Vincent College, notes "advocating viewpoints which are opposed to Catholic dogma and the official pronouncements of the Holy See on issues of faith and morals (not the presentation and critical discussion of viewpoints)." Others refer to "Unchristian conduct and false doctrine" or "undermining the faith or morals of students." One Roman Catholic college gives as a grave reason "civil divorce, instituted by the faculty member."

In returning to a general view of the nature of termina-

[38] The second of these phrases led the Project to ask for elaboration; in reply the president said "I find myself somewhat at a loss to explain. . . . When the provision was written we probably had in mind the fact that the college is church-related. . . ." and then goes on to say that no issue has arisen on this ground during his sixteen-year experience.

tion criteria, caution must be exercised in order to avoid too exact an equating of the literal language of a standard and its actual application. In short, the relationship of bark to bite. Any experienced teacher in higher education knows how various—and sometimes erratic—will be the imposition of adverse judgments. An act of dissent, at one place and time, will be favorably regarded as evidence of a stalwart, independent spirit; elsewhere, on another day, the same act might be damned as gross insubordination. In an institution which states that "tenure will continue as long as the faculty member maintains satisfactory scholastic and personal standards . . . [and] sound professional relations . . ." it is doubtful whether either the administration or the teachers can have a clear understanding of the practical effect of such language.

Termination because of Financial Exigencies

The propriety of terminating a tenure appointment "under extraordinary circumstances because of financial exigencies" is recognized in the 1940 "Statement of Principles." The questionnaire replies indicate that in twenty-nine institutions reduced income, lack of demand for courses, or major curricular or departmental revision might lead to termination of service even for teachers with tenure. The most detailed statement of this policy encountered is that of Haverford College:

It is recognized that, while no drastic changes in curriculum or in general program are now planned, it is possible that emergency conditions, such as war, or major changes in demand for instruction or in the social or economic environment, might require changes in college policy that would make unwise and uneconomical the continuance of certain

49

fields of instruction. Where circumstances affect the demand for certain courses, or certain courses are eliminated from the curriculum, the President shall exert every effort to make suitable adjustments in teaching assignments and personnel. In the event that it is not practicable to find employment in another department or in another capacity for a faculty member affected by such adjustments, his contract may be terminated by the college even though he has academic tenure. In such a case, two years' notice of such termination shall be given with full salary during this period.

Six institutions indicated adherence to the following statement taken from the 1925 "Conference Statement on Academic Freedom and Tenure":

Termination of permanent or long-term appointments because of financial exigencies should be sought only as a last resort, after every effort has been made to meet the need in other ways and to find for the teacher other employment in the institution. Situations which make drastic retrenchment of this sort necessary should preclude expansions of the staff at other points at the same time, except in extraordinary circumstances.[39]

Five stated that tenure termination because of financial exigencies would be by seniority (at one college by seniority within departments).

The questionnaire replies do not indicate that termination of tenure because of financial exigencies is or has been a significant problem. The reason probably is that there are so many other less drastic means of meeting a financial crisis than the extreme measure of dismissing a teacher

[39] See Appendix C for a brief account of the origin and present status of the 1925 "Conference Statement."

with tenure. Thus, in event of financial need, all salaries could be reduced by a fixed percentage instead of placing the burden on a small group of teachers who are singled out for dismissal; two institutions reported that this technique of a general percentage reduction was employed during the depression. Or faculty members could be encouraged to seek positions at another college or university, or in nonacademic employment. Or, applying the principle of seniority, the contracts of nontenure appointees might not be renewed instead of dismissing teachers with tenure.

It thus is difficult to conceive of situations which would require dismissal of teachers with tenure because of financial exigencies. But since the future cannot be foreseen it probably is prudent to recognize that financial problems may arise and that possibly the extreme expedient of dismissal would have to be utilized. Plans so stating should afford the teacher affected an opportunity of a hearing before a faculty committee. Most important, whether or not there is specific provision for dismissal because of financial need, tenure plans should provide for consultation with a properly constituted faculty group concerning any financial problem which might seriously prejudice faculty members with tenure.

Procedures for Termination

Due process in our civilization has firmly established itself as the controlling idea in the administration of justice under law. And the force of this principle has extended itself so widely that many other kinds of action by which society arrives at a judgment have fallen under its influence. One example of this extension is found in the procedures by which academic tenure may be terminated. The term "academic due process" is now in common use.[40]

However, the principle of due process and its practice are probably a good deal closer to each other in the law than in nonlegal procedures. For one thing, the law knows that it has the responsibility of ultimate judgment; other judgments—for example, a decision by an educational institution to terminate a tenure appointment—may turn out to be preliminary, subordinate, and eventually subject to judicial assessment. Also, courts have been developing the idea of due process over hundreds of years; academic due process is at the beginning of its life.

Academic due process has been further conditioned in its development by the special qualities of higher education, regarded as a social institution. First, one must reckon with the customs of fraternal association and with the sense of community of scholarship which are present in some degree on every campus. These elements of spiritual sustenance affect teachers profoundly. One result is that teachers, who live by intellectual freedom, are not avid for rules—even good ones. Second, many colleges and universities operate under a historical, ethical, or religious tradition characterized by intelligence and discrimination; teachers at such institutions understandably feel themselves well protected even in the absence of procedural safeguards. Finally, teachers—like other persons of common sense—know that the existence of a procedure is not a certain guarantee of justice; more than one blameless man has been hanged by due process.

[40] See *Academic Due Process*, a policy statement of the American Civil Liberties Union prepared by that organization's national Academic Freedom Committee (1954); reprinted in *AAUP Bulletin* 42: 655–661 (1956); reprinted here in Appendix F.

The last general reservation is a truism but one which bears emphasis. In all procedural matters there is always the problem of the spirit and the letter—the paradox of the poor rule intelligently adapted to a serious situation, or inversely the good rule patently neglected or misused.

Fifty of the eighty institutions here studied offer some statement about procedure for termination of tenure. Although there is great variety in the procedures described, and conspicuous gaps in many of them, four distinct areas of procedural action emerge:

Procedure for informal adjustment and conciliation.
Procedure preliminary to, and in preparation for, a formal hearing.
Procedure by which the hearing body is constituted.
Procedure in the formal hearing and subsequent procedure relating to decision and appeal.

Procedure for informal adjustment and conciliation. It would seem self-evident that both the college or university administrators and the teacher who confront a question of tenure termination would be well advised to sit down together and discuss their common problem. In some instances, clarification of the facts or the positions taken by the parties may resolve the issue; there are always situations in life which result mainly from ignorance or misunderstanding. For example: an administration might not know about a heavy personal burden carried by a teacher, a burden not created by his own weakness but nonetheless adversely affecting his work. Or a teacher might through misunderstanding or confusion rather flagrantly fail to observe the proper balance between devotion to classroom duties and research. In such situations, if there is any good will present, it should be possible to reach a solution before lines of opposition and conflict have a chance to develop.

Should the issue persist, there is at least the further hope that the institution and the teacher can arrive at a genuinely equitable agreement about the terms of parting. Admittedly, principles must be fought for in many such situations. But some institutions and some teachers will, if only for protection of their reputations, agree to a not too unsatisfactory severance.

The procedure for informal adjustment and conciliation should of course reflect the fact that in such sessions the administration is present as a party, with power, bringing charges; and the teacher is present as a party, without power, making a preliminary defense. This difference in vantage point, and this inevitable adumbration of an adversary situation, cannot be avoided. It does mean, however, that from the first word spoken the administration should demonstrate a scrupulously fair and ethical attitude.

At this beginning, informal stage, when specific charges have not yet been formulated, it is important that the teacher be told that he is free to discuss the matter but that he is not under any compulsion to make a statement or to respond to questions. Until the issues have become clarified and the teacher has been given an opportunity to refresh his recollection in light of the specific charges, there is a danger that in the course of a random discussion ill-considered statements will be made. One way to avoid this risk would be to assure the teacher that the discussion was merely exploratory and that nothing said at the session would be presented as evidence at a later formal hearing. Another protective device would be for the teacher to be represented by counsel at the meeting. The specific safeguard to be utilized is not as important as the general proposition that at this preliminary point in the proceedings it is unfair to put the teacher in the position of either responding to general allegations or having adverse inferences drawn from a failure to respond.

In this first phase of what may develop into an action terminating tenure, it would seem particularly desirable that all concerned should discipline themselves and keep the matter private. Although privacy in such matters is not an end in itself, or unquestionably desirable in every instance, it is an important consideration for the reputation of the teacher, the good of the institution, and the peace of the community. More than one case history indicates that an issue of possible termination has been magnified into irreconcilable conflict when the public appetite for a good fight is stimulated by premature revelation.

The usefulness of procedure for informal adjustment and conciliation has been argued in a priori terms, contrary to the usual analytical approach of this study, for the reason that so mildly reasonable a procedure is stated to exist at only five of the eighty colleges and universities. Of course some institutions probably provide for informal discussion of termination through their general rules for handling matters of common concern to administration and faculty. Unfortunately, it is exactly those general provisions which seem to have a way of being avoided or misapplied when the question of termination casts its first somber shadow.

Of the five institutions which provide such procedure, Roosevelt University has by far the most detailed. Among other matters, this institution states that after such a preliminary discussion "each person present may file with the President and with all concerned his own record of the discussion." [41]

Procedure preliminary to, and in preparation for, a formal hearing. A hearing on a tenure-termination issue in an educational institution is essentially a trial, even though it is not conducted in a courtroom. Like any other defendant in a trial, the teacher should be given notice of the charges against him. He should also be informed concerning the evidence which will be used to support those charges, be provided with a set of the rules which will govern the hearing, and be assured of the right to counsel. These protections are needed from the start—during the period of preparation for the hearing as well as during that event.

Twenty-five of these eighty colleges and universities state that the teacher will receive written charges. It is difficult to understand why this figure is so low when one considers the virtually absolute necessity for written charges in the preparation of an adequate defense. Without them the trial of specific points and appeal upon questions of fact or academic principle can hardly hope to be intelligent, much less successful.

Two of the eighty institutions commit themselves to presenting the teacher with a summary of the evidence to be introduced at the formal hearing; no institution states that it offers a list of the witnesses to be called by the administration. Perhaps some of this information would be embodied in the written charges, where such are offered, but there is no assurance.

Not one institution among the eighty explicitly states that it will give the defendant a full portfolio of the rules

[41] "Constitution of the Faculty," Art. V, Sec. 2, Clause 4.

relating to the constitution of the hearing body and to the hearing procedure.[42] Some teachers will perhaps be successful in digging out what they need to know by an examination of relevant legislation, charter provisions, bylaws, administrative regulations, and faculty legislation. Some may be assumed to have the help of adequate counsel for this job. Nevertheless, failure to provide such information certainly constitutes a burden, if not a handicap. As a matter of fact, all concerned would benefit by being fully informed about applicable standards and rules; if both parties understand how business is to be done, it will be much easier to give early and chief attention to the merits of the case.

The very poor showing with regard to procedure prior to formal hearing is extremely disheartening. In most places, it seems, the teacher may very well get off to a bad start. Of course, as has been noted with regard to other deficiencies, one may assume that some institutions are in practice more generous than their silence indicates. Generosity, however, is not an adequate substitute for a stated right in matters of professional life and death.

Procedure by which the hearing body is constituted. Forty-six of the eighty colleges and institutions provide for a hearing by some kind of group. Possibly the dividing line is less numerically exact when it comes to practice; and a judgment concerning a particular institution must take into account the actual incidence of termination cases. Thus, one large private university states that it has no standing procedure; but this deficiency should be viewed in the light of the fact that no termination cases have arisen there

[42] Roosevelt University in effect supplies much of this information by embodying it in its faculty constitution.

in the past ten years and that responsible faculty opinion believes "conditions of academic freedom may be considered as very good." A smaller college states that, although there are no official procedures, practice conforms to the 1940 "Statement of Principles" and no cases have arisen in ten years; here, however, responsible faculty opinion characterizes the tenure situation as "between bad and indifferent."

Of the forty-six hearing groups twenty-one are faculty committees. Of these, twelve are standing, seven are *ad hoc*, and two are not described. With respect to personnel, twelve of the faculty committees are stated to be drawn from the faculty at large, and four others are probably so derived; six are not characterized. The obvious advantage of a standing over an *ad hoc* committee is the likelihood of its members having been selected prior to and without relation to a particular termination case which may come before it. On the other hand, faculty standing committees of all kinds sometimes become inactive through disuse—even to the point of fossilization—and may not necessarily provide, at a particular point in time, the best possible personnel for an important judgment.

Six of the twenty-one faculty hearing committees are expressly said to have only an advisory function. But the reserve power of most governing boards in a sense makes this true of the findings of any group or person whose judgment the board has the ultimate power to review.

Examination of the procedure by which the twenty-one faculty committees are set up reveals that at eleven places selection is by faculty choice, and at three by administrative appointment. Consequently, at the seven other institutions which provide for a faculty committee, the absence of a stated procedure for selection might at the outset lead to disagreement on the collateral issue of the manner in which the hearing group comes into being.

The second most numerous type of hearing group, fourteen in number, is the governing board itself; sometimes this is the whole body, sometimes a board committee. Two of these institutions require that the hearing before the board shall be in the presence of a faculty committee.

There are a variety of mixed committees: faculty-board (6), faculty-administration (4), administration-board (1), and faculty-administration-board (2). The effectiveness of such joint committees would probably have to be determined by a study of their work in actual termination cases. But their composition is at least open to the same general objections which were noted in regard to mixed groups acting on the acquisition of tenure. What is needed is independent faculty judgment, whatever the fate of that judgment may be in later proceedings. And in the termination of tenure, even more than in the granting of tenure, there is doubtful wisdom—even possible danger—in asking teachers to sit jointly with other persons who have a higher authority.

The possibility of a divisive spirit in the mixed committees is recognized, even emphasized, in three institutions. Two of these have a 2-2-1 make-up; two persons are chosen by the faculty, two by the administration, and the fifth is elected by the other four. One faculty-administration committee has a member chosen by the teacher whose case is being reviewed, a member named by the faculty, a member named by the administration, and the president and dean.

The danger in selecting committees in this fashion is that the members may tend to think of themselves as representing the group from which they are appointed or the person who selects them. The hearing and decisional processes may become less a dispassionate search for facts and the exercise of objective judgment and more a process of conciliation and compromise. Although such a procedure may be appropriate in handling labor disputes, it is unsuited to the work to be done by a committee considering termination of tenure in an educational institution.

One place provides a hearing only before the administration. Needless to say, such a procedure flatly contradicts the concept of a college as a community of self-selecting and self-assessing scholars.

A summary view of the procedure governing the make-up of the hearing body is disappointing if there is expectation of something like "judgment by one's peers." Although more than half of the eighty institutions provide for a hearing group, in only twenty-one will judgment be rendered by a faculty committee, and only twelve of these committees are standing and thus free from the potential bias inherent in *ad hoc* creation. This is a poor showing. It may account for the fact that so many termination cases have as part of their record serious dissatisfaction with the personnel of the hearing group.

Procedure in the formal hearing and subsequent procedure relating to decisions and appeal. The American legal tradition places great emphasis on the principle that the accused is entitled to know the case against him, to confront and cross-examine adverse witnesses, and to present evidence and argument to an unbiased tribunal. Notwithstanding the importance of these procedures as a means of ascertaining facts and contributing to a just result in tenure-termination cases, it has been urged that confrontation and cross-examination should not be guaranteed, because some witnesses may be embarrassed or even harmed. Thus, the argument has been advanced that a female student who has charged a male teacher with improper sexual advances would be loath to confront him at a hearing and, if required to do so, might even suffer trauma. Perhaps so, and certainly every device of considerate propriety should be used to protect such a witness. But life frequently presents hard choices. And it would seem the part of justice—and justice, not delicacy, is the issue—to attach greater importance to a man's whole career than to the sensibility of a witness. Such would be the rule in a court of law. An educational institution should not adopt a less just rule, although it might apply it less formally.

It is also sometimes suggested that it is unnecessary for the teacher being tried to hear all the evidence and argument, because he is in the good hands of responsible people, trained in scholarly objectives, who may be trusted to weigh the allegations and opinions of the very few witnesses who for one reason or another should not be open to challenge. The weakness in this view is that the hearing is much more than an investigation. It is an "adversary proceeding" in which two parties will contend about the serious matter of justice for a human being. In such a proceeding it is the right to challenge that discloses which is the truth among "truths." It is the right to challenge that permits opinion about the credibility of the witnesses. There are enough possible mistakes in adjudication without adding to their number by denying the right of confrontation.

A number of specific procedures supporting the right of confrontation are sporadically stated in the tenure plans examined, but it is evident that such procedures have not been widely adopted. Of course, many colleges and universities may follow such procedures in particular cases, as a matter of intelligence or fairness.[43] The specific procedures are these:

1. THE RIGHT TO BE PRESENT. The right of the teacher to be present throughout the hearing is stated by only four of the eighty institutions. Surely so elementary a right is more widely respected than this figure indicates; perhaps, even, the right to attend one's own trial has been regarded as too obvious to require notice. Nevertheless, the fact remains that it could be denied in seventy-six places.

2. THE RIGHT TO SEPARATION OF PROSECUTORY AND JUDICIAL FUNCTIONS. A trial in a court of law, in the United States, requires virtually complete separation of the prosecutory and the judicial functions. On the other hand, in government administrative hearings of a quasi-judicial nature there is considerable variety in the degree of differentiation; nearly always an official of the agency involved brings the charges, but the hearing group may be merely other officials sitting together for that special purpose or officials who constitute a permanent hearing group or even a detached quasi-judicial body. In noneducational private employment, every kind of system operates—from joint sessions of the management and the union grievance committee to simple discharge at the order of the boss.

As noted above, only eleven of the eighty institutions place the teacher on trial before a faculty committee chosen

[43] In the detailed presentation which follows, these procedures are set forth in terms protective of the teacher; it should be understood that they would equally protect the institution. For example, both parties should have the right to cross-examine, the right to prompt adjudication, etc.

by the faculty. In all the other colleges and universities the influence of the administration—which brings the charges —could directly or indirectly affect the hearing group. The most direct influence would exist in situations where administrative officers sit on the tribunal. Indirect influence might exist where the administration appoints all or some of the faculty members who will hear the case.

Roosevelt University offers the most explicit procedure for dissociating the administration, when it is a party in interest, from the hearing group. There, tenure-termination cases, like other major grievance matters, in time come before the Executive Committee of the Senate; this body of nine includes the President and the Dean of Faculties, ex officio, and one dean, three heads, and three staff members all elected by the faculty. The following significant regulation comes into play:

The hearing (if any), the finding, and the recommendation shall be entrusted to a panel of the Executive Committee from which panel the following shall have been eliminated: the President, any Dean who has heard the case, any party to the dispute, anyone who by majority vote of the Executive Committee is disqualified because of interest or expressed bias. If a qualified panel cannot be secured by this means, vacancies on the panel shall be filled by selecting members of the Executive Committees of the College Councils by lot.[44]

3. THE RIGHT TO COUNSEL. Only twenty of the institutions indicate that a teacher may have counsel present at the formal hearing. Two restrict his choice to colleagues, and at neither of these institutions is there a law faculty.

[44] The provision for exclusion of interested administrative officers is the basis for classifying the hearing group at Roosevelt as all-faculty and faculty-chosen.

63

A defendant without counsel of course labors under a severe handicap.

4. THE RIGHT TO CROSS-EXAMINE. The principle of confrontation necessarily embodies full opportunity for cross-examination. Unfortunately, the assurance of this right is limited. Only four of the eighty institutions stated its existence, in response to inquiry; and of these four only one institution indicates this right in an official regulation. Reversing the figures, teachers at seventy-six of the eighty colleges and universities cannot know or assume that they will have the right, in a hearing involving their professional career, to test the evidence brought against them.

Two possible limitations affecting cross-examination are significant enough to warrant particular notice. The administrative head of one major institution, commenting informally and tentatively, feels that cross-examination of oral testimony would be in order, but that "if the evidence against [the teacher] . . . were written, it would seem to me that revealing the witness's identity at the hearing would need the writer's consent." Such a procedure would gravely limit the right of cross-examination; it might even encourage personally hostile individuals to present adverse evidence in writing as a way of escaping the cross-examination which would reveal their animus. The rule should, it seems, go in the reverse direction—and require that unidentifiable evidence be inadmissible.

The other limitation, which is made explicit in the tenure plan of Roosevelt University, restricts the right to cross-examine to the parties personally and specifically denies this opportunity to counsel. Perhaps the basis for such a restriction is the understandable fear that lawyers will "take over" and introduce complexities unsuited to a hearing

PLANS AND PRACTICES

within an educational institution. But this risk should perhaps be endured for the sake of other desirable elements
of a trial. Objectivity, for instance, might be diminished if
the parties conduct the cross-examination; either an ac-
cuser or a defendant, confronted by a witness adverse to
his position, might quite understandably find his personal
feelings affecting his questioning. Also, neither the administration nor the defendant may possess the necessary
professional skill for effective cross-examination.

5. THE RIGHT TO PRESENT AND "SUMMON" WITNESSES.
The right to present witnesses at the hearing is assured by
six of the eighty institutions. In addition, seven institutions
offer a limited right by their general acceptance of the 1940
"Statement" which says: "In the hearing of charges of
incompetence the testimony should include that of teachers
and other scholars, either from his [the teacher's] own or
from other institutions."

The right to "summon" witnesses is a necessary com-
plement of the right to present witnesses. Typically, neither
the institution nor the teacher has actual subpoena power.
The institution, however, does have authority over its
own staff; such persons would find it difficult to refuse to
appear if called by the administration. Fully developed due
process would likewise offer the teacher the use of the
authority of the institution, whatever its limits might be,
for his needs in calling witnesses. It is not enough for him
to be able to count on those who will voluntarily support
him by an appearance. He must also be able to produce
witnesses who are timorous or even hostile, if he believes
their testimony will be helpful.

Only two institutions appear to endorse this right. Wilson College states that the teacher "shall have the privilege

of calling his own witnesses to appear before the Education Committee [of the board]." Roosevelt University says that "parties have the right to call witnesses in any hearing." These statements, embodied in official publications, at least imply assistance by the authority of the institution. They appear to be the only examples of "subpoena" power available to the teacher among the eighty institutions.[45]

6. THE RIGHT TO AN AVAILABLE FULL RECORD. Another fundamental element in due process is the creation of a full record of the hearings and its availability to both parties. Nine of the eighty institutions require that a full record shall be made. The same nine indicate that it shall be "available" to the teacher, but the several contexts rather clearly suggest that availability means no more than that it shall be open to inspection. One institution, Roosevelt University, permits the teacher to have physical possession but only under special conditions: "Except by unanimous consent of all concerned, no one but the President shall have the right to buy or retain the verbatim reports."

Here, fortunately, practice appears to be somewhat better than the statement of right. The experience of such organizations as the American Association of University Professors and the American Civil Liberties Union indicates that the record is frequently made available to the teacher and to outside agencies with a responsible interest.

No institution states that it will provide the teacher with a record at its expense.

There are a number of possible explanations for this possessive attitude toward the record by the administrators

[45] An official of a major Pennsylvania institution offers the following comment: "I do not see how the school could assist him by subpoenaing witnesses for him without putting itself in the position of prejudicing the outcome of the hearing."

of an educational institution. Fear of assisting a possible future legal action against itself, fear of publicity, a desire to protect witnesses, are all probably operative. But for the teacher the result can be painfully serious. At a later date in his career he may be asked to explain some aspect of his earlier ordeal or even to give a relatively full description of the proceedings. Presumably he can draw on the statement of charges, the findings, and the judgment; his recollection and his personal notes will help him; but this is not enough. If he is to be fair to himself, to the witnesses, and to the tribunal, he will need to be able to refer to the full transcript of the record.

7. THE RIGHT TO PROMPT ADJUDICATION. Prompt adjudication is a significant element in academic due process, both for the ordinary reason that a difficult situation should not be prolonged and because a teacher under charges is paralyzed with regard to looking for employment elsewhere. But only four of the institutions surveyed indicate awareness of the importance of expeditious determination.

At La Salle College, a teacher receiving notice of dismissal has five days in which to request a hearing, and this hearing must be held within ten days after his request. At Roosevelt University the hearing must be held within two months; a two-month postponement may be requested by either party, and when both agree further postponements are possible; if there should be delay in the appellate proceedings, the teacher may take his case directly to the governing board when eight months have elapsed since the original hearing. Bradley University and the University of Chicago do not fix specific time limits, but other references to the chronology of events create the impression of reasonable expedition.

8. THE RIGHT TO APPEAL PROCEDURES. Appeal by a teacher

from an adverse decision is explicitly provided for in seven of the eighty institutions; such appeal may variously be taken to the president or the governing board. In the seven places that provide for appeal, the scope of the review is not stated except by one institution in which the board review is a complete *de novo* trial. The general absence of any detailed information about appeal procedure is not unexpected in the light of the poorly developed due process structure in the prior phases of termination action.

Lincoln University is unique in providing that judgment of a faculty-administration-board hearing committee shall be final. The faculty bylaws, approved by the board of trustees, state:

After the presentation of the charges, he shall have the privilege of a hearing before a judicial committee consisting of two members of the respective faculty affected, appointed by the President; two non-administrative members of the University Faculty elected by that Faculty, and one member of the Board of Trustees, appointed by the Chairman of the Board. This committee shall be constituted at the first Faculty meeting of each academic year. The decision of the full committee shall be final.[46]

SUMMARY

The stated plans and practices which have been reviewed yield a picture of mixed deficiency and completeness, clarity and confusion. If these eighty institutions are at all typical of American colleges and universities, tenure sys-

[46] The text of the bylaw continues: "At his own option, the person in question may, when charges are first brought, appeal directly to the Board of Trustees. In making such an appeal directly to the Board of Trustees, the person in question shall forfeit the right to trial by the Special Committee."

tems in higher education present a wide range in degree of perfection, and the poorest of them are notably defective in providing a sound relationship between the teacher and the institution.

With regard to acquisition of tenure, sixty-nine of the eighty colleges and universities confer tenure automatically after a probationary period or when a particular rank is reached. Eight confer tenure in practice. Only twenty-four, however, provide for automatic acquisition at any rank after a probationary period—the system endorsed by the American Association of University Professors and the Association of American Colleges in their joint 1940 "Statement of Principles."

Evaluative criteria for acquisition of tenure are stated at half the institutions, but the standards are set forth in language which suggests a semantic jungle. Only a few places offer systematic exposition and reasonably precise phraseology.

Procedures governing acquisition of tenure are found in three-fourths of the colleges and universities surveyed. Only twenty-six of the eighty, however, provide for faculty action in granting tenure. Appeal from denial of tenure is a stated right at thirty-five institutions, but only thirteen call for a faculty judgment in this proceeding.

With regard to criteria for the termination of tenure, more than half of the institutions indicate incompetence as a specific cause, and about the same number designate immorality. Nine of the eighty name as a cause some failure in institutional relationship.

Termination procedures are clearly the weakest element in the whole tenure picture.[47] Although fifty of the colleges

[47] See the "Statement on Procedural Standards in Faculty Dis-

and universities offer some description of procedure, most of the essential safeguards of academic due process have only scattered representation, and some are virtually nonexistent.

Due notice has been taken of the fact that serious weaknesses in the completeness and quality of standards and procedures may in fact be ameliorated by good practice and thus result in fair treatment of some individuals. Nevertheless, to the degree that the weaknesses are present, bad practice can the more readily result, with consequent unfair treatment of other individuals.

---

missal Proceedings," adopted in 1958 by the Association of American Colleges and the American Association of University Professors "as a guide" but not as a "norm." The "Statement" is reproduced in Appendix E.

III

Tenure and the Law

AS stated at the outset, the essential characteristic of tenure is continuity of service, in that the institution in which the teacher serves has in some manner, either as a legal obligation or as a moral commitment, relinquished the freedom or power it otherwise would possess to terminate the teacher's services.[1] The concept of tenure as a legal obligation calls for a brief discussion of the meaning and significance of legal enforcement of a right to tenure. This is followed by an analysis of the various legal problems presented by the plans and practices summarized in Chapter II.

LEGAL ENFORCEMENT OF TENURE

In a state-financed, as distinguished from a "private," college or university, the teacher who has been dismissed in violation of the tenure plan would most likely seek to secure a court order directing the governing board to reinstate him. The reasoning supporting issuance of such an

[1] Page 2 above.

71

order would be as follows: The tenure plan promulgated by the governing board is a form of sublegislation which has the force and effect of law; a discharge contrary to law is outside the board's authority; the court should uphold and enforce the law by ordering the board to reinstate the teacher.[2]

The legal position of a teacher with tenure who is wrongfully discharged by the governing board of a private institution may be quite different. Conventional legal analysis would say that his right to tenure is contractual—that is, one of the terms of the contract between the teacher and the institution is that the teacher will not be dismissed except as provided in the tenure plan. A dismissal which violates the tenure plan would constitute a breach of contract by the institution. The usual legal remedy for breach of contract is a judgment for money damages. The general formula for computing the amount of the judgment is that the injured party should be awarded a sum sufficient to put him in the same position he would have been in had the contract been performed. A teacher with tenure who is wrongfully dismissed would thus be awarded an amount equal to that which he would have received from the institution, less whatever income he earned (or reasonably could have earned) from similar work which the dismissal enabled him to undertake. After a judgment has been entered, the law's remedy for nonpayment is the sale of the defendant's assets by the sheriff or other official and payment of the proceeds of the sale to the plaintiff in satisfaction of his judgment.

[2] See *State ex rel. Keeney* v. *Ayers*, 108 Mont. 547, 92 P.2d 306 (1939); *State ex rel. Richardson* v. *Board of Regents*, 70 Nev. 144, 261 P.2d 515 (1953), 70 Nev. 347, 269 P.2d 265 (1954); Newton Edwards, *The Courts and the Public Schools* (1955), 508.

The usual remedy for breach of contract thus is a judgment for money damages rather than a specific order directing the defaulting party to perform the contract. In some cases, however, the law will enter an order directing the defendant to perform his promise and in event of noncompliance with the order will fine or imprison the defendant for contempt of court. An order of specific performance of the contract will be entered where the usual "legal remedy is inadequate," i.e., where a judgment for money damages is not the substantial equivalent of the promised performance.

A court might with reason conclude that money damages are not an adequate remedy for the teacher with tenure who has been wrongfully deprived of the opportunity to continue his career of teaching and research in the institution of his choice. It does not follow, however, that a specific order of reinstatement would be issued. For there is another legal principle which says that even though the legal remedy is inadequate the court will not decree performance of a personal service contract. The theory underlying this doctrine is that neither party to the contract should be compelled to maintain the undesirable personal relations that performance of the contract would require and that enforcement of the decree would impose too great a burden on the court.[3] Although the rule against enforce-

[3] It is possible, although highly unlikely, that a similar limitation to judicial enforcement may be found to exist with respect to a state institution. For it is sometimes said that mandamus is "equitable" in character and that the court may refuse to issue a writ of mandamus in its sound discretion. Thus, if the discharged teacher should petition a court for mandamus order to reinstatement, it is conceivable that the judge might say that in light of the particular facts the writ should not issue, because its issuance would result in intolerable personal relations between the petitioning teacher on

ment of personal service contracts has been circumvented in a few instances, the decided cases offer little basis for confident prediction that the teacher wrongfully discharged by a private institution would secure a judicial order of reinstatement.[4]

The foregoing emphasizes an important limitation of legal enforcement of tenure: in private institutions the wrongfully discharged teacher may have no legal right to reinstatement. There are other drawbacks, such as the expense and delay incident to judicial vindication of a right to tenure, the difficulty of proving money damages to the degree of certainty that the law requires, the fairly wide scope of discretion retained by the institution in most tenure plans, the understandable reluctance to litigate publicly one's fitness as a teacher or scholar, and the fact that too often in times of stress courts tend to reflect community prejudices.

It is thus apparent that assurance of continuity of employment extended by an institution with a long and honorable tradition of academic freedom and tenure often will be much more meaningful than an express legal obliga-

---

the one side and the administrators, faculty, or student body on the other.

[4] Consult Zechariah Chafee, Jr., Sidney P. Simpson, and John P. Maloney, *Cases on Equity* (1951), 281 n. 40; Harold C. Havighurst, *Cases and Materials on the Law of Contracts* (1950), 171–172; *Jones* v. *Williams*, 139 Mo. 1, 39 S.W. 486, 40 S.W. 353 (1897); *Restatement of the Law of Contracts* (1932), § 379; A.L.R. Annot. 135: 279 (1941).

A recent case upholding injunctive relief against threatened dismissal in a public school situation is *Lemasters* v. *Willman*, 281 S.W.2d 580, (Mo. App. 1955), discussed in Robert R. Hamilton and E. Edmund Reutter, *Legal Aspects of School Board Operation* (1958), 112.

tion grudgingly assumed by a lesser institution. To this extent, Robert M. Hutchins was right when he stated, "[T]he issue of legal control is not basic. Academic freedom comes and goes because of some conviction about the purpose of education on the part of those who make the decisions in society." [5] But Russell Kirk, although he may have somewhat overstated the case, also had an important point when he said, "The courts, when all is said, remain the chief defense of academic freedom when a right to tenure . . . can be proved." [6] For tenure enforceable in law does have certain advantages over tenure which rests on a legally uncontrolled discretion of governing boards. The availability of judicial review of an order of dismissal can operate as a curb on the occasional arbitrary administrator or governing board. The fact that the teacher has legally enforceable rights may strengthen the hand of the conscientious administrator or trustee when inflamed public pressures unjustifiably seek the discharge of a teacher. Most important, the existence of a disinterested tribunal to resolve differences, when all efforts to do so amicably have failed, removes the teacher from the demeaning position of dependence on a governing board's benevolence and contributes to the creation of a milieu of independence and freedom in which a scholar can work most effectively.

Essentially the same considerations which have caused the demise of benevolent despotism as a system of political government argue against vesting unrestrained power in administrative or trustee groups in academic government. As Madison so well said, "If men were angels, no govern-

[5] Robert M. Hutchins, "The Meaning and Significance of Academic Freedom," *The Annals* 300: 72, 76 (1955).

[6] Russell Kirk, *Academic Freedom* (1955), 71.

ment would be necessary." [7] So, in the case of teachers' tenure: although the wisdom and uprightness of administrators and trustees may provide a primary safeguard, "experience has taught . . . the necessity of auxiliary precautions." [8] In academic government one important "auxiliary precaution" is legally enforceable tenure.

The fact that legal enforcement is a significant, although not necessarily determinative, aspect of a faculty member's right to tenure accounts for inclusion in this study of the more important legal issues presented by the various plans and practices. Let it be noted, however, that although the study should be helpful to members of the legal profession who may represent institutions or teachers in tenure matters, there is no intention to provide a treatise of the law of tenure. The purpose is, rather, to furnish information and appraisal which may assist the three groups most directly involved—trustees, administrators, and faculty members—intelligently to discharge their responsibilities in establishing and maintaining sound conditions of creative scholarship in American higher education.[9]

[7] *The Federalist*, No. 51.   [8] *Ibid.*

[9] Since this study deals with tenure plans and practices established by trustees, administrators, and faculty, we do not consider the separate but related problem of restrictions on academic freedom and tenure—e.g., loyalty oaths—imposed by public legislative bodies such as state legislatures or municipal councils. For interesting discussion of the constitutional aspects of such restrictions, see Arthur E. Sutherland, "The American Teacher's Freedom and Responsibility," *J. Soc. Pub. Teachers of Law*, 3: 220 (1956); Thomas I. Emerson and David Haber, *Political and Civil Rights in the United States* (1952), 848–876, "Constitutional Protection of Academic Freedom." And see *Sweezy* v. *New Hampshire*, 354 U.S. 234 (1957).

ACQUISITION OF TENURE

Three of the eighty colleges and universities studied stated that there were no formal or informal provisions for acquiring tenure. In these institutions, the absence of even an informal tenure policy underscores the unlikelihood of administrative or trustee protection of the tenure principle. The same lack would most likely render recourse to the courts futile. In this group, then, tenure in any meaningful sense probably does not exist either in law or fact.

The remaining seventy-seven institutions replied that some measure of tenure was recognized, either formally in a governing document—such as statutes, bylaws, or manual—or informally as a matter of unwritten practice.[10] In these institutions tenure has some significant measure of *de facto* existence. For it is to be assumed that administrators and trustees who have formally or informally provided for acquisition of tenure would not lightly abandon or restrict the policy so declared. Institutional recognition of tenure—whether expressed formally in governing documents or informally as a matter of policy—also provides a strong ethical base for internal and external professional support of

[10] The breakdown is as follows: 27 institutions stated that the tenure plan was included in the statutes, bylaws, or plan of government; 20 others replied that the plan was expressed in a statement which had been approved or adopted by the governing board; in 9 the plan appears in a document promulgated by the administration, such as a faculty manual, but apparently not explicitly approved by the governing board; in 2 the plan is set forth in the faculty constitution, with no indication of governing board action; 5 institutions offered a formal definition of tenure but did not indicate a source; and 14 indicated that although tenure was informally recognized, its incidents were not spelled out in a formal document.

77

a professor's rights in event of infringement of the tenure principle.[11]

But despite the fact that the vast majority of administrators and trustees may be expected to adhere to formal or informal expressions of tenure policy, there have been in the past, and undoubtedly will be in the future, instances of basic disagreement between the institution and the teacher. In such a case the teacher may wish to have the controversy resolved by the courts. If he is successfully to invoke the "command of the public force [which] is intrusted to the judges," [12] he must be prepared to show that the formal or informal provisions for acquisition of tenure created a legally enforceable obligation. Under the present state of the law, he must, in "private" institutions at least, convince the court that the provisions for tenure are part of a valid contract between him and the institution.[13]

[11] See Mark H. Ingraham, "Academic Freedom—The Role of the Professional Societies," *Proceedings of Amer. Phil. Soc.* 101: 441 (1957).

[12] The phrase is that of Justice Holmes, "The Path of the Law," *Harv. L. Rev.* 10: 457 (1897), reprinted in *Collected Legal Papers* (1920), 167.

[13] In "public" institutions the teacher could supplement the contract argument by pointing to holdings that tenure rules promulgated by governing boards of "public" universities have the "force of law" or the "force and effect of statute." *State ex rel. Keeney* v. *Ayers*, 108 Mont. 547, 556, 92 P.2d 306, 310 (1939); *State ex rel. Richardson* v. *Board of Regents*, 70 Nev. 144, 150, 261 P.2d 515, 518 (1953).

Richard Hofstadter and Walter P. Metzger, *The Development of Academic Freedom in the United States* (1955), 460–462, has an interesting discussion of early (and unsuccessful) attempts to induce courts to hold that professors had a "freehold" in their office of which they could not be deprived without notice and hearing. See below, p. 138, for a recommendation that in some instances a court should feel free to hold that a teacher has a legally protecti-

An initial obstacle to acquisition of legally enforceable tenure will be found in the charters of some institutions. Most of the colleges and universities included in the study operate under charters granted by the legislature. Many of the charters contain specific provisions concerning the appointment and removal of teaching personnel. Some of these provisions state that the trustees may "remove . . . any of the instructors . . . as said Trustees shall deem the interest of said University requires,"[14] or remove teachers "at their discretion, as the welfare of the Institution may demand,"[15] or "remove them at will."[16]

---

ble interest which may be said to rest on *status* rather than on contract.

[14] Section 10 of the charter granted to Lake Forest College in 1857.

[15] Section 6 of the charter granted to Thiel College in 1870.

[16] Article 4 of the charter granted to Pennsylvania Female College (now Chatham College) in 1869.

These examples were taken from the 19 charters forwarded with the questionnaire replies. Additional relevant removal provisions from these charters follow: Allegheny College, § 10, "to remove them for misconduct, immorality or breach of the laws and rules of the institution" (charter granted in 1817); Blackburn College, § 1, "remove them from office" (1857); Bucknell University, Art. II, § 4, "removing them for misconduct, breaches of the ordinance of the institution, or other sufficent causes" (1846); Dickinson College, Art. VI, "removing them for misconduct, or breach of the laws of the institution" (1783); Geneva College, § 8, "removing the members thereof as occasion may require" (1883); Gettysburg College, § 8, "censuring or removing them for incapacity, inattention to duty, for breaches of the ordinances and rules of the said Institution or other conduct which the Trustees shall deem sufficient ground therefor" (1832); Illinois College, § 7, "displace and remove . . . the instructors . . . as said trustees shall deem the interest of the said college shall require" (1835); Lafayette College, Art. VI, "removing them for misconduct, breaches of the ordinances of the institution or other cause which shall be deemed suf-

A number of courts have held that provisions of this kind "deprived the governing board of power to make a contract with a teacher for any definite term . . . and that attempts by it to do so were wholly nugatory in a legal sense." [17] If the approach of this group of decisions were followed, the teacher with tenure who is dismissed in violation of the terms of the tenure plan would have no legal redress whatsoever. He could secure neither a judgment for damages nor a judicial order reinstating him to his position.

Other courts have given this type of provision a less drastic effect, holding that although such a clause empowers the governing board to remove the teacher at any

ficient" (1826); Lehigh University, Art. VIII, "removing them for misconduct, neglect of duty or breach of the laws of the institution or for any reason they, the majority, may deem sufficient" (1866); University of Pittsburgh, § 4, "removing them for misconduct" (1819); Rockford College, § 3, "remove any of them for sufficient reasons" (1847); and Lebanon Valley College, § 5, "removing them after an impartial trial for immorality, neglect of duty or incompetency" (1867)

Other examples may be found in Edward C. Elliott and M. M. Chambers, *Charters and Basic Laws of Selected American Universities and Colleges* (1934): Knox College, § 4, "remove either of the instructors, officers or agents, as they may deem the interests of the College require" (1837); Northwestern University, § 6, "displace any or such of them as the interest of the Institution may require" (1851); Stanford University, Art. Fifth (2) of the "Grant Founding and Endowing the Leland Stanford Junior University": "It shall be the duty of the Trustees to give to the President of the University the following powers: . . . (2) To remove professors and teachers at will."

[17] See discussion and citation of cases in *Cobb* v. *Howard University*, 106 F.2d 860, 864 (C.A.D.C.), cert. denied, 308 U.S. 611 (1939); Hofstadter and Metzger (note 13 above), pp. 465–466; Note, "Academic Freedom and the Law," *Yale L.J.* 46: 670, 672–673 (1937); Edward C. Elliott and M. M. Chambers, *The Colleges and the Courts* (1936), 81–85.

time, "it does not deprive the board of the power to make binding contracts for reasonable terms." [18] Under this view the wrongfully dismissed teacher might recover damages for breach of the tenure contract but could not secure an order of reinstatement.

The less restrictive interpretation of the second group of decisions is clearly preferable. As noted by Justice Valentine in an early Kansas case:

It would certainly be for the interest of the college that the board should have such power. No man of spirit, of self-respect, and of capability, would want to hold an office or position at the whim or caprice of a body of men with whom he might have but little if any personal acquaintance. . . . The shorter and more precarious the tenure of the office, the less attractive, important and valuable it would be; and generally, men of only inferior talent could be found to accept it or to perform its functions with such a precarious tenure.[19]

These considerations are strong arguments in support of the less drastic approach, and they should be sufficient to convince a court faced with the task of interpreting such a charter provision. Unfortunately, there is a very serious risk that the court would not find the arguments persuasive and would therefore follow the other line of precedents, said to be the "majority" view.[20] There is also danger that

[18] Note, "Contract Rights of Teacher Discharged from Educational Institution Incorporated under Special Statute," *Ill. L. Rev.* 35: 225, 226 (1940). See also materials cited in note 17 above; *United Producers and Consumers Co-operative* v. *Held,* 225 F.2d 615 (C.A. 9, 1955); *In re Paramount Publix Corporation,* 90 F.2d 441, 111 A.L.R. 889 (C.A. 2, 1937).

[19] *Board of Regents* v. *Mudge,* 21 Kan. 223, 230 (1878).

[20] That this is a real and not a fanciful risk is borne out by two recent cases: *Posin* v. *State Board of Higher Education,* 86 N.W.2d

a court would hold that, while the charter provision permits the institution to make *reasonable* contracts with its teachers, a contract for *lifetime* employment is not reasonable. And it is obvious that under either interpretation the court would be powerless to issue a specific order of reinstatement, even if other applicable legal doctrines would have allowed its issuance.[21]

These are risks and burdens which teachers should not be expected to bear, particularly in the light of the "increasingly greater emphasis [which teachers are placing on] provisions for tenure," [22] and the fact that only a very, very small percentage of teachers in institutions with such charter provisions could be expected to know of their existence, much less to understand their legal significance.

The teacher who seeks legal enforcement of a tenure contract must not only be prepared to establish that the institution had power under its charter to enter into the contract but, of equal or greater importance, he must also prove that the institution did in fact make such a contract. In a few institutions the letter of appointment (or promotion) states specifically that the appointment is subject to the "rules of tenure now in effect" or to the "provisions of the Statutes of the University." [23] In such instances the

31 (N.D. 1957); *Worzella* v. *Board of Regents,* Sup. Ct. of South Dakota, Dec. 10, 1958. The "majority" view reference is from the *Ill. L. Rev.* Note cited above, note 18.

21 See text discussion at note 3 above.

22 See comment of Justice (then Judge) Rutledge in *Cobb* v. *Howard University,* 106 F.2d 860, 865 n.21 (C.A.D.C.), cert. denied, 308 U.S. 611 (1939): "It is common knowledge that teachers, in seeking academic connections at the collegiate level, lay increasingly greater emphasis upon provisions for tenure. . . ."

23 Roosevelt University and University of Chicago.

The letter of appointment of Muhlenberg College states, "All contractual arrangements are, of course, subject to provisions stipu-

formal rules of tenure in the bylaws or other governing document are made part of the contract between the teacher and the institution.[24] The questionnaire replies indicate, however, that such an express incorporation term is not customary and that letters of notification often state only that the recipient has been appointed or promoted to a particular rank. If the bylaws in fact provide that the rank in question carries tenure, the problem presented is whether such tenure provisions became part of the employment contract.

If the teacher has knowledge of the bylaw provisions, there is good reason to conclude they become part of the contract between him and the institution.[25] It may also be urged that the same result should be reached "irrespective of whether the teacher is aware of . . . [the bylaws], since they are matters of public record and he is presumed to know them." [26] Another mode of reaching the same con-

---

lated by the by-laws." The letter of reappointment of Lincoln University states, "You will further note that the terms stated in this letter are subject to ratification by the Board of Trustees of Lincoln University, and are otherwise subject to the conditions set forth in the Constitution and By-laws of the Board of Trustees and the Faculty of Lincoln University (Statutes) that govern relationships between the University and instructional employees."

[24] *State ex rel. Keeney* v. *Ayers*, 108 Mont. 547, 92 P.2d 306 (1939); *Backie* v. *Cromwell Consol. School Dist.*, 186 Minn. 38, 242 N.W. 389 (1932).

[25] *University of Mississippi* v. *Deister*, 115 Miss. 469, 76 So. 526 (1917); accord, *Board of Education* v. *Cook*, 3 Kan. App. 269, 45 Pac. 119 (1896); *Board of Regents* v. *Mudge*, 21 Kan. 169 (1878).

[26] Elliott and Chambers (note 17 above), p. 76. See also *Cobb* v. *Howard University*, 106 F.2d 860, 863 (C.A.D.C.), cert. denied, 308 U.S. 611 (1939); *People ex rel. Kelsey* v. *New York Post-Graduate Medical School and Hospital*, 29 App. Div. 244, 248, 51 N.Y.S. 420, 422 (1st Dep't 1898); *Trustees of the University of Alabama* v. *Walden*, 15 Ala. 655, 658 (1849).

clusion would employ the reasoning that, in the language of the law, there is an "ambiguity" as to the remaining terms of an employment relation created by a letter of appointment which states only that the recipient has been appointed to a particular rank at a stated salary. It is always appropriate to resolve an ambiguity by reference to relevant documentary data. Here the relevant data would be found in the bylaws or other governing document.[27]

It is entirely possible, of course, that an institution would advance the argument that the bylaws merely expressed the policy or intention of the institution but did not create a legally enforceable obligation. This argument should not be accepted. Not only would the institution "be in an absurd position if it challenged the force of its own by-laws" [28] but, in the absence of a clause expressly disclaiming an intent to create legal relations, it is reasonable to conclude that the tenure provisions were intended to be legally enforceable.[29] Notwithstanding, it must be recognized that there is a risk a court would not be persuaded and would, instead, agree with the contention that the tenure rules were simply an expression of intention.

The teacher's burden would be considerably more oner-

[27] Arthur L. Corbin, *Contracts* (1951), III: 110.

[28] *Ironside* v. *Tead*, 13 N.Y.S.2d 17, 21 (Sup. Ct. 1939), modified mem., 258 App. Div. 940, 17 N.Y.S.2d 994 (1st Dep't), aff'd mem., 283 N.Y. 667, 28 N.E.2d 399 (1940).

[29] See cases cited above, note 26. Note especially the statement of Justice (then Judge) Rutledge in the *Cobb* case, quoted above, note 22. And consider *Wilson* v. *Rudolph Wurlitzer Co.*, 48 Ohio App. 450, 454, 194 N.E. 441, 443 (1934): "It is plain that the pension plan was an integral part of the program for his employment. To say that it constituted merely a nebulous inducement, unsupported by an intent to be bound by the provisions mentioned, is to charge the employer with the grossest fraud."

ous if the bylaws or other governing document which provided for tenure also disclaimed an intention to create legal
obligations. For example, the statement "Faculty Tenure
and Academic Freedom" adopted by the Board of Trustees
of Knox College on June 11, 1949, begins:

> The Trustees declare the following policy in regard to
> faculty tenure, *without implication that it involves any con-*
> *tractual obligations:* [emphasis supplied]

There follow detailed provisions for acquisition of tenure
which, in the absence of the italicized disclaimer clause,
would be sufficient to create contractual obligations on the
part of the College. Does the disclaimer clause negate the
contractual relations which otherwise would exist?

The answer of orthodox contract law in all likelihood
would be that the disclaimer clause did negate contractual
relations. Judicial rationale of this conclusion would probably be expressed in language similar to that employed by
Lord Justice Atkin in a leading case involving a similar
problem:

> To create a contract there must be a common intention of
> the parties to enter into legal obligations, mutually com-
> municated expressly or impliedly. Such an intention ordi-
> narily will be inferred when parties enter into an agreement
> which in other respects conforms to the rules of law as to
> the formation of contracts. It may be negatived impliedly by
> the nature of the agreed promise or promises, as in the case
> of offer and acceptance of hospitality, or of some agreements
> made in the course of family life between members of a
> family. . . . If the intention may be negatived impliedly it
> may be negatived expressly. In this document, construed as
> a whole, I find myself driven to the conclusion that the
> clause in question expresses in clear terms the mutual inten-

85

tion of the parties not to enter into legal obligations in respect to the matters upon which they are recording their agreement.[30]

It should be noted, however, that "when the subject matter of an agreement is of a kind that is customarily dealt with in enforceable contracts, and the parties have in fact acted under the agreement, a court is likely to look with some distaste at provisions which seem to exclude all legal sanction and remedy." [31] And there are cases, principally in the field of employees' pension and bonus plans, in which courts have interpreted disclaimer clauses so as to make them ineffective.[32]

Thus it is possible, but not likely, that if the Knox disclaimer clause—or a similar clause in other tenure plans [33]—

[30] *Rose and Frank Co. v. Crompton Bros., Ltd.,* [1923] 2 K.B. 261, 293 (concurring opinion), rev'd on other grounds, [1925] A.C. 445; accord, *Bradley v. New York University,* 124 N.Y.S.2d 238 (Sup. Ct. 1953), aff'd, 283 App. Div. 671, 127 N.Y.S.2d 845 (2d Dep't.), mem., 307 N.Y. 620, 120 N.E.2d 828 (1954) (Trustee statement on academic freedom and tenure stated, "[T]his is a statement of policy and not a draft of a contract. . . ." Said the court, "[T]he express language . . . clearly shows that it did not create any binding obligation upon the University." 124 N.Y.S.2d at 242); *Spooner v. Reserve Life Insurance Co.,* 287 P.2d 735 (Wash. 1955), 44 Geo. L.J. 145. Cf. *Cobb v. Howard University,* 106 F.2d 860, 862 n.8 (C.A.D.C.), cert. denied, 308 U.S. 611 (1939).

[31] Corbin, *Contracts* (1950), I, § 34.

[32] Note, "Legal Status of Private Industrial Pension Plans," *Harv. L. Rev.* 53: 1375, 1379–1380 (1940); A.L.R.2d Annot. 42: 461, 468 (1955).

[33] The "Faculty Rank and Tenure Policy" of an institution in Pennsylvania whose questionnaire reply requested that it not be identified begins with the following statement: "(The Rank and Tenure Policy of the University, revised after a year's trial, is herein stated. As a Policy, it is a settled course adopted by the institution with respect to the field of rank and tenure. As a Policy, it does not have the binding force of a contract, but is susceptible

were litigated, the court would hold that legal relations had been created. Some support for such a conclusion may be found in the fact that the Knox clause does not clearly, expressly, and affirmatively disclaim legal liability on the part of the College. The clause does not, for example, state that the "tenure policy hereby announced is not intended to and does not create any liability whatsoever on the part of the College," or that the "tenure plan herein outlined is a gratuity and creates no legal obligation." It might be urged, therefore, that inclusion of the provision, "without implication that it involves any contractual obligation," was not designed to negate all legal liability, but was designed to reserve to the College power to make reasonable changes in the plan as experience thereunder demonstrated the need or desirability of amendment.[34] Ancient canons of contract construction supply makeweight support for this more limited interpretation of the clause.[35]

At best, the presence of a disclaimer clause in a tenure plan creates uncertainty, for the teacher will not know whether he has acquired tenure protected by law until after the plan has been the subject of litigation. At worst, the disclaimer clause defeats legal enforceability. To in-

---

to revision by the University when circumstances would cause such a settled course to become unsettled, or when it becomes evident that such a settled course is not leading to the desired goal.)"

[34] See below, pp. 115–117.

[35] Doubts arising from ambiguity of language are resolved against the party using it. 2 Bl. *Comm.* *380; Bacon, "Maxims of Law," in *Tracts* (2d ed. 1741) 42. An interpretation which renders an agreement valid will be preferred to one which makes it void or its performance meaningless. *Vestry of Shoreditch* v. *Hughes,* 17 C.B. (N.S.) 137, 162, 144 Eng. Rep. 55, 65 (C.B. 1864). An interpretation of a contract which would lead to a forfeiture will not be favored. Samuel Williston, *Contracts* (rev. ed. 1936), III, § 620.

clude a disclaimer clause in a tenure plan is in effect to say to the teachers in the institution: "We recognize the importance of tenure in maintaining and promoting proper principles of academic freedom and therefore we announce the following tenure rules. But these 'rules' really aren't rules; they are merely an expression of present intention. We reserve the right, when the chips are down, to do as we think best. We are unwilling to subject our interpretation to review by an independent judiciary, the instrumentality established by society to adjudicate disputes. If this is unacceptable to you, you may go elsewhere." All the reasons advanced in Chapter I to justify tenure in institutions of higher learning, as well as the discussion in the introductory paragraphs of this chapter on the advantages of legally enforceable tenure, argue against the paternalism which, in some kind or degree, lies behind disclaimer clauses.

Fortunately, disclaimer clauses rarely have been included in formal tenure plans. Therefore the consequences of the clauses, uncertainty and possible legal unenforceability, are not major problems in terms of the number of teachers affected. Unhappily, however, the same shortcomings may be found in other tenure programs which do not contain disclaimer clauses.

There is, first, a small number of tenure plans which, although not containing express disclaimer clauses, include ambiguous terms or provisions which give rise to serious question whether enforceable legal relations have been created. The situation at Drexel Institute of Technology is illustrative. In 1934 the trustees provided for employment on "indefinite tenure." In a 1954 faculty meeting the president described a new plan for appointment to "indefinite tenure." Article VI of the bylaws adopted in 1947 (and contained in a document bearing a 1954 publication date) states that teachers "hold their offices during the pleasure of the Board of Trustees." Letters of appointment or promotion to positions of "indefinite tenure" also state that the recipient shall hold office "during the pleasure of the Board [of Trustees]." [36] A similar condition appears to exist at Illinois College. There tenure is recognized and letters of appointment to positions of tenure expressly state that the appointment carries tenure.[37] But Article VII of Illinois College bylaws, entitled "Rank and Term of Appointment . . . of Faculty," provides:

The initial appointment of Professors shall be for one year, after which term they may be given permanent appointments of indefinite term, *it being understood that the term of appointment may be terminated by either party to*

[36] Compare the statement adopted by the Board of Trustees of Bucknell University. After providing for tenure, the statement continues: "The Trustees, while recognizing the moral obligations set forth in the preceding paragraphs, retain the full responsibility imposed upon them by law and the Charter of the University to exercise their own judgment from time to time as occasion requires, through such agents as they choose, so far as the employment of professional personnel to run the university is concerned."

And see Article VI, 4, of the bylaws of Wilson College: if a professor's appointment is "renewed, the appointment shall be for long term or without limit of term and shall be construed as establishing, in general, a reasonable expectation of permanency in full time service to the college." Millikin University states, "Except for grave moral delinquency or gross incompetence, a member of the faculty on indefinite tenure shall not be dismissed without notice given at least five months prior to the end of the college fiscal year."

[37] "It is a pleasure to inform you that the Board of Trustees at its meeting of [date] acted officially approving your appointment as Professor of [department] with tenure."

the contract upon reasonable notice. . . . [emphasis supplied]

The initial appointment of Associate Professors shall be for one year. They may thereafter be appointed for terms of three years, with permanent tenure possible after one three-year term, at the discretion of the President and the Faculty Committee. . . .

Teachers at these institutions who seek judicial protection of their alleged right to tenure might be successful. But they might also find that the "pleasure of the Board" authorized removal at will [38] or that termination upon "reasonable notice" means that the power to remove is limited only by a requirement of giving notice reasonably in advance of the date of removal. Unlike disclaimer clauses, which reflect a deliberate attempt to withhold the sanction of the law, the defects of these plans may be the accidental result of poor draftsmanship.

Troublesome issues of uncertainty and legal unenforceability also inhere in "informal" tenure plans. These are programs for tenure which exist in practice but which have not been formally expressed in the bylaws or other governing document. In these institutions if the academic freedom and tenure tradition is deep and strong and if the trustees, administrators, and faculty are enlightened and courageous, the teacher's tenure will, in all likelihood, be amply protected. But here, as in the disclaimer clause situation, disagreements may arise and the teacher may wish to invoke the aid of the courts. To do so successfully, he must show that he acquired tenure. Most courts probably would hold

[38] *People ex rel. Kelsey* v. *New York Post-Graduate Medical School and Hospital,* 29 App. Div. 244, 51 N.Y.S. 420 (1st Dep't. 1898). (Conflict in bylaw provisions similar to Drexel conflict authorized removal at will.)

that he must prove that the institution's tenure practices—even though not formally expressed in governing documents—are a part of the contract between him and the institution. This task would be greatly facilitated if the plan were described in reliable documents which could be subpoenaed or otherwise made available to the court. These might include minutes of trustees' meetings, data supplied by the institution to accrediting organizations, addresses by the president to meetings of the faculty, and other similar written or transcribed statements.

Unavailability of documentary proof of the tenure plan would not necessarily defeat the teacher's claim to legal protection, for responsible administrators or others might give oral testimony from which the existence of a provision for tenure might be inferred. But if the existence and terms of the tenure plan must be proved by oral testimony, the way of the teacher will be hazardous. Conflicts in testimony may result; the details of the plan may not be proved with sufficient definiteness to permit judicial enforcement; and the fact that the plan has not been reduced to writing may lead the judge or jury to conclude that the "plan" is not contractual but is merely a general expression of institutional policy devoid of legal significance.[39]

[39] Informal plans might also be denied legal recognition because of a failure to comply with the Statute of Frauds, cf. *Brookfield* v. *Drury College,* 139 Mo. App. 339, 123 S.W. 86 (1909), or because administrative officials lacked authority to adopt a tenure plan, cf. *Sittler* v. *Board of Control,* 333 Mich. 681, 53 N.W.2d 681 (1952); *Trustees of State Normal School* v. *Wightman,* 93 Colo. 226, 25 P.2d 193 (1933); *Auburn Academy* v. *Strong,* 1 Hopkins (N.Y.) 278 (1824). See also *Thomas* v. *Catawba College,* 104 S.E.2d 175 (N.C. 1958). (Tenure plan authorized dismissal for adequate cause and provided for payment of at least a year's salary if dismissal did not involve moral turpitude; plaintiff was dismissed

A final item bearing on legal enforceability of tenure deserves comment—not because of its intrinsic difficulty or significance but because it has been the subject of mis-understanding in lay and legal circles. Under the typical tenure plan, the institution which has given a teacher in-definite or continuous tenure must continue the teacher's appointment until his death, retirement, or dismissal for adequate cause or because of a bona fide financial exigency. The teacher, on the other hand, is not committed to re-main at the institution until death, retirement, or dismissal. He may resign at any time; his only obligation is to make his resignation effective at the end of the school year and to give reasonable notice in advance.[40] This one-sidedness of the relationship has caused a few trustees and adminis-trators to express doubt that an institution could reasonably be expected to assume such an unfair, unilateral obligation and an occasional judge to assert that the arrangement lacks "mutuality" and therefore is legally unenforceable.[41]

---

and was paid his salary for a year thereafter; the court held that plaintiff's acceptance of the salary constituted an "election of rem-edies" which barred him from maintaining this action for wrongful discharge.)

[40] Tenure plans do not usually require faculty members to give advance notice of intention to resign. The plan of Temple Uni-versity is a significant exception: "The members of the faculty agree that, in fairness to the University, they will not resign or in any other manner terminate their services until they have first given to the University the fullest possible notice in order to spare the University embarrassment, and to give it an opportunity to appoint proper substitutes." See *Sylvan Crest Sand & Gravel Co.* v. *United States*, 150 F.2d 642 (C.A. 2, 1945) (requirement to give notice found by "implication"). And see the "Statement Concern-ing Resignations, 1929," *AAUP Bulletin* 42: 46 (1956).

[41] E.g., Morris, J., dissenting in *State ex rel. Keeney* v. *Ayers*, 108 Mont. 547, 92 P.2d 306 (1939).

Viewed abstractly, the relationship is one-sided. But there is no principle of law or morals that mutual promises must be coextensive. Numerous decisions may be found in the law reports upholding agreements which bind one party but permit the other to terminate the arrangement at his option.[42] A typical instance of such an agreement is the case of an employee who, having been injured because of the alleged negligence of his employer, promises not to sue the employer in return for the employer's promise to provide lifetime employment; the employee, like the teacher with tenure, does not promise that he will remain in the employer's service for life. The courts regularly hold that notwithstanding the employee's power to terminate the arrangement at any time, the employer is required to provide lifetime employment.[43] In legal terms, the employee's forbearance to sue is consideration for the employer's promise to provide lifetime employment. Similarly in the case of a teacher's tenure contract, the teacher's service at the institution, or his action in leaving another school and coming to the institution as a tenure appointee, or, perhaps, his express or implied agreement to give reasonable notice before resigning, provides the consideration needed to make the institution's tenure promise enforceable.[44]

[42] Corbin, *Contracts* (1950), I, §§ 161–164; Williston, *Contracts* (rev. ed., 1936), I, § 141; and see *Rague* v. *New York Evening Journal Publishing Co.*, 149 N.Y. Supp. 668, 164 App. Div. 126 (2d Dep't 1914).

[43] E.g., *F. S. Royster Guano Co.* v. *Hall*, 68 F.2d 533 (C.A. 4, 1934); and see A.L.R. Annot. 135: 646 (1941).

[44] See *State ex rel. Anderson* v. *Brand*, 303 U.S. 95 (1938); *Kostanzer* v. *State ex rel. Ramsey*, 205 Ind. 536, 187 N.E. 337 (1933); *State ex rel. Keeney* v. *Ayers*, 108 Mont. 547, 92 P.2d 306 (1939); *Stevens* v. *G. L. Rugo & Sons, Inc.*, 209 F.2d 135, 139 n.2 (C.A. 1, 1953); *Luchacher* v. *Kerson*, 158 Pa. Super. 437, 45 A.2d 245

The only question of consequence is whether the promise of tenure is in fact part of the bargain between the teacher and the institution. The fact that tenure is an important buttress of the principle of academic freedom, to which all colleges and universities express adherence, and that, as Justice (then Judge) Rutledge pointed out in the *Cobb* case, "teachers in seeking academic connections at the collegiate level lay increasingly greater emphasis on provisions for tenure" [45] are adequate reasons for the conclusion that in the absence of a disclaimer clause the provisions of formal tenure plans are part of the bargain between the teacher and the college or university in which he serves.

CRITERIA FOR TERMINATION OF TENURE

The heart of any tenure plan is the limitation it imposes on the authority the institution otherwise would possess to terminate a teacher's services. Thus a fundamental issue is the meaning to be given to the criteria for termination set forth in the particular plan. What is meant by "adequate cause," "just cause," "misconduct," "incompetence," and the other more explicit criteria of the various programs summarized in Chapter II?

Judicial precedent does not yield precise answers to these questions. The scarcity of authoritative decisions is due in large part to the fact that "only isolated cases involving teachers in institutions of higher learning have reached the courts." [46] Equally important is the circum-

---

(1946), aff'd, 355 Pa. 79, 48 A.2d 857 (1946); *Littell* v. *Evening Star Newspaper Co.*, 120 F.2d 36 (C.A.D.C., 1941); A.L.R. Annot. 135: 646 (1941).

[45] See note 29 above.

[46] Emerson and Haber (note 9 above), p. 889.

stance that when such cases have been presented, they have usually been decided on grounds other than interpretation of termination criteria. Most of the cases decided after the Civil War and before World War I, for example, upheld the principle that "trustees and regents, unless the statutes provided to the contrary, were empowered to dismiss professors at will." [47] There is, however, a cluster of court cases interpreting termination criteria in tenure plans of American colleges and universities which it may be helpful to consider.[48]

An early and historic decision involved Dr. James Murdock, professor of ecclesiastical history in the Theological Institution of Phillips Academy.[49] The constitution of the Theological Institution authorized removal "for gross neglect of duty, scandalous immorality, mental incapacity, or any other just and sufficient cause."

The charges brought against Dr. Murdock in 1827 were (1) that there were in his mind "jealousies of the other members of the faculty . . . and a want of confidence in his colleagues . . . tending to the material injury, if not

[47] Hofstadter and Metzger (note 13 above), p. 465; and see Note, "Academic Freedom and the Law," *Yale L.J.* 46: 670, 673 (1937): "[M]ost courts have denied recovery of damages for breach of contract even where dismissal was unjustified. . . ."

[48] Additional enlightenment concerning judicial interpretation of termination criteria may be found in the rather large number of cases construing termination clauses in statutory tenure plans for public primary, secondary, and junior college teachers. See, e.g., Edwards (note 2 above), pp. 481 ff.; Robert R. Hamilton and F. Edmund Reutter, Jr., *Legal Aspects of School Board Operation* (1958), 67–70.

[49] *James Murdock, Appellant from a Decree of the Visitors of the Theological Institution in Phillips Academy*, 24 Mass. (7 Pick.) 303 (1828), *Murdock v. Phillips Academy*, 29 Mass. (12 Pick.) 244 (1831).

the prostration, of the government of the institution";
(2) that there was a "wide and settled difference of views
between Dr. Murdock and the trustees in regard to the
arrangement in relation to his department"; (3) that he
had criticized his colleagues before students, had criticized
one colleague to another, "with the design of prejudicing
that one against the other"; and had "disclosed the proceedings and differences of the faculty in their official meetings,
in such communications impugning the opinions and acts
of his colleagues"; and (4) that he had failed to deliver lec-
tures as required by the trustees' regulations and had failed
to criticize student compositions, also as required by the
regulations.[50]

The Massachusetts court held that the fourth charge
stated facts and circumstances which constituted gross neglect of duty and justified Murdock's dismissal. But, said
the court, the first three charges would not justify dismissal,
for they "are of so indistinct a character, that they hardly
wear the appearance of offences, being the effect, if true,
rather of constitutional infirmities of temper and disposi-
tion, than of perversity of mind or criminal intention." [51]
Chief Justice Parker's discussion of these charges is note-
worthy in two respects. It emphasizes that differences in
opinion between teacher and colleagues or between teacher
and trustees "unaccompanied by . . . actual existing mis-
chief" do not warrant dismissal, and it points out that
"advice and admonition" or even "severe admonition"
would be "preferable to the exercise of that final act of
power which separates the accused from his associates and
deprives him of his living." [52]

[50] 24 Mass. (7 Pick.) 308–309.   [51] 24 Mass. (7 Pick.) 330.
[52] 24 Mass. (7 Pick.) 330, 331.

Nearly a hundred years later the opinion of the Supreme Court of Missouri in *Darrow* v. *Briggs* [53] reflected a wholly different approach. Under its original charter a majority of the Board of Trustees of Drury College was required to profess the faith and creed of the Congregational Church; later, apparently in order to secure Carnegie retirement benefits, the charter was amended to prohibit sectarian tests. Professor Fritz Darrow was employed as professor of Biblical Greek in September, 1907. Darrow was a member of the Universal Brotherhood and Theosophical Society and in December, 1909, donated a book, *Key to Theosophy*, to the local city library. At this juncture a local Methodist minister took up the cudgels against this "atheist," "scatter-brained" professor, who "has either an ill-balanced intellect, or else is evilly disposed." [54] Darrow replied in an article in a local newspaper. The battle raged in pulpit and press until the summer of 1910, when the trustees voted that Darrow's term of office should terminate on September 1, 1910.

The Supreme Court of Missouri upheld the termination, saying in part,

[We] are unable to conceive of the avowal by a college teacher of devotion to a cult such as Theosophy and a taking up in a newspaper controversy of the cudgels in defense thereof, being anything but hurtful to any college. . . . We do not think there is any doubt that the voluntary acts of plaintiff, as he himself pleads them, of themselves furnished ample cause for his dismissal, and that Drury College violated

[53] 261 Mo. 244, 169 S.W. 118 (1914) (action for breach of contract; according to Darrow's petition, the bylaws authorized removal "when in the judgment of . . . [the] board the interest of the college shall require it").

[54] 261 Mo. at 259, 261, 262, 169 S.W. at 120, 121.

97

no contract when it dismissed him. It is beside the question that he may have been dragged, or nagged, as counsel charge, into his unfortunate attitude by the officious intermeddling of a pragmatic zealot.[55]

Other decisions sanctioning discharge have been made: by the Illinois Appellate Court, which held that De Paul University, a Catholic institution, could terminate the appointment of an apostate priest who had concealed his apostasy when he was employed to teach German in the University; [56] by the Supreme Court of Errors of Connecticut in the case of the academic dean of Larson College, who wrote critical—said by the court to be "defamatory"—letters concerning the college president to parents of students in the college; [57] and by the United States District Court for the Western District of Missouri in the case of a teacher at the University of Kansas City who refused to answer questions put to him by University officials concerning membership in the Communist Party.[58]

Occasionally resort to the courts has been successful. The most notable victory was won by University of Ne-

[55] 261 Mo. 273–274, 169 S.W. 124.
[56] *Fuller* v. *De Paul University*, 293 Ill. App. 261, 12 N.E.2d 213 (1938), *Ill. L. Rev.* 32: 986 (1938) (action for breach of contract; held, intentional concealment justified discharge).
[57] *Breen* v. *Larson College*, 137 Conn. 152, 75 A.2d 39 (1950) (action for breach of contract; held, breach of implied "duty of good faith and loyalty" justified discharge).
[58] *Davis* v. *University of Kansas City*, 129 F. Supp. 716 (W.D. Mo., 1955) (tenure plan provided that services of teachers with tenure could be terminated "only for adequate cause, except in the case of retirement for age or because of financial exigencies"; held by Judge, now Justice, Whittaker, refusal to answer constitutes adequate cause for dismissal). See also "The University of Kansas City," *AAUP Bulletin* 43: 177–195 (1957).

vada Professor Frank Richardson in 1954.[59] Dr. Richardson, "a mild-mannered and amiable ornithologist," [60] who had been at Nevada for eleven years, held an appointment with tenure, and was head of the department of biology, president of the Nevada chapter of the American Association of University Professors, and chairman of the faculty committee on scholastic standing. He opposed the relaxation in admission policies which the new president, Dr. Minard W. Stout, apparently favored. Dr. Richardson distributed about thirty copies of an article, "Aimlessness in Education," written by Arthur E. Bestor, professor of history at the University of Illinois, and published in the *Scientific Monthly*.[61] The article was critical of "professional educators"; President Stout was a doctor of education. Dr. Richardson also stated at a meeting of the local chapter of the American Association of University Professors on February 18, 1953, "I am surprised to see so many here in view of the unfair and unwarranted criticism of the A.A.U.P. made by the president this afternoon." [62] At an earlier meeting in the president's office Dr. Stout had informed Dr. Richardson that he was "hired to teach biology and not to be a buttinsky all over the campus." [63]

The controversy continued until, on March 31, 1953, President Stout wrote Dr. Richardson that he should ap-

[59] *State ex rel. Richardson* v. *Board of Regents,* 70 Nev. 144, 261 P.2d 515 (1953), 70 Nev. 347, 269 P.2d 265 (1954). See also "Academic Freedom and Tenure: The University of Nevada," *AAUP Bulletin* 42: 530 (1956); "The University of Nevada: An Appraisal," Nevada Legislative Counsel Bureau, Bulletin 28: 27–31 (1957).

[60] Kirk (note 6 above), p. 60.

[61] *Scientific Monthly* 75: 109–116 (Aug., 1952).

[62] 70 Nev. 356, 269 P.2d 270.

[63] Kirk (note 6 above), p. 65.

pear for a hearing before the Board of Regents on April 10 to show cause why he should be continued as a member of the faculty beyond June 30, 1953. The letter enumerated "disturbing activities" in which it was alleged Dr. Richardson had participated. These activities were "the attempt to develop friction between departments on the campus [and] . . . between the University and public schools of the state"; "the spreading of false information to infer the abolishment of many faculty committees . . . [and] to infer the lowering of academic standards at the University . . . [and] to infer the maltreatment of faculty members by the administration"; and "the alarming of faculty, townspeople, and legislators without first presenting the matter to the administration or to the Faculty Welfare Committee." [64]

Counsel for Dr. Richardson sought and, with the aid of the Supreme Court of Nevada, secured a bill of particulars. The hearing before the Board of Regents was held May 25–27. Russell Kirk describes the attitude of the Regents as follows: "One of the Regents subsequently remarked that though it was a pity to lose Dr. Richardson, it would have been worse to have lost Dr. Stout; another, an aspirant after the gubernatorial chair of Nevada, was hotly opposed to any compromise." [65] After the hearing, the board made the following finding: "The Board determines that Dr. Frank Richardson has demonstrated insubordination, that he has not been cooperative and that his conduct has not

[64] Kirk (note 6 above), p. 66. The tenure rule provided, "A staff member under tenure shall be removed only for cause and after a hearing before the Board of Regents." 70 Nev. 144, 146, 261 P.2d 516.

[65] Kirk (note 6 above), p. 68.

been in accord with the welfare of the University." [66] On the basis of this finding the board entered an order removing Dr. Richardson as a member of the faculty.

The Supreme Court of Nevada vacated the board's order. After dismissing some of the matters as "trivial," the court stated that the propriety of the dismissal hinged on the charges in the bill of particulars that Dr. Richardson (1) had asserted that the president had made an unfair attack on the American Association of University Professors and (2) had distributed the Bestor article. In answer to the contention that Dr. Richardson had made "false accusations against the president," the court held that Dr. Richardson's statement before the local chapter of the Association was clearly a statement of opinion which he was entitled to express and which could not have misled his hearers. The court concluded its discussion of this phase of the case in language strongly reminiscent of that used by Chief Justice Parker in the *Murdock* opinion over a century before:

But assuming for the sake of argument that there was some degree of impropriety or lack of taste in Dr. Richardson's remarks in opening the A.A.U.P. meeting, we have no hesitancy in concluding, in view of Dr. Richardson's history and record at the University, that it did not of and in itself constitute cause for removal.[67]

The court then turned to the argument that distribution of the Bestor article was an attack on the president and the department of education and therefore constituted "insubordination," which the court defined as conduct which "imparts a willful disregard of express or implied direction,

[66] 70 Nev. 355, 269 P.2d 269.   [67] 70 Nev. 358, 269 P.2d 271.

or such a defiant attitude as to be equivalent thereto." [68] After a most detailed examination of the evidence, the court found that distribution of the Bestor article was not an attack on the president or the education department but was, instead, a permissible expression of views on a subject in which the members of the faculty had a legitimate interest. The court concluded, "[T]he record presents no substantial support of either the finding of insubordination or the finding of lack of cooperation and presents no cause for removal." It therefore vacated the order of removal.[69]

Whatever significance this small group of cases may have is not primarily the enlightenment they provide concerning the precise meaning of criteria for terminating tenure. The number of factual situations is much too limited to permit fruitful generalizations, and it may be doubted that some of the decisions will prove to be persuasive precedents.[70] More important than their narrow holdings is the proposi-

[68] 70 Nev. 367, 269 P.2d 276.

[69] See also *Colorado School of Mines* v. *Neighbors*, 119 Colo. 399, 203 P.2d 904 (1949). (Neighbors, assistant coach from 1937 to 1945, was appointed director of physical education for the 1945–1946 school year. To supplement his princely salary of $2,750 per annum, Neighbors managed the "cocktail lounge in the LaRay Hotel." In February, 1946, the School discharged Neighbors because he refused to terminate his hotel employment. In a suit by Neighbors for the salary he would have earned during the remainder of the 1945–1946 school year, the court stated that "moral justification did . . . attend the action of the trustees," but held that the trustees were not legally justified in refusing to pay him his salary. However, because Neighbors earned from other sources an amount in excess of that which he would have earned had he not been discharged, he was awarded only nominal damages.)

[70] The *Drury College* case, particularly, is questionable; and one may doubt, also, whether the *Neighbors* case has seminal significance.

tion, emphasized by both Chief Justice Parker in the *Murdock* case and by Justice Badt in the *Richardson* case, that differences of opinion between teacher and administrators do not justify termination of a tenure appointment. Also significant are Chief Justice Parker's recognition of the gravity of the dismissal sanction—in his terms, "the final act of power which separates the accused from his associates and deprives him of his living"—and his observation that the lesser sanctions of "admonition" or "severe admonition" often would be sufficient.[71] Most important is the proposition implicit in both opinions that judgment concerning a teacher having tenure should be based not on an isolated act of alleged misconduct but on the individual's entire record as a teacher and scholar.[72]

The meaningful issue of judicial interpretation of termination criteria thus is not so much one of judicial precedent as of approach and attitude. The judge who understands the importance of academic freedom in American higher education, who perceives the relationship of tenure to the maintenance and protection of that freedom, and who, like

[71] This assumes, of course, that the teacher's conduct warrants imposition of any sanction.

[72] For further discussion of this principle, see "Report of the Committee on Academic Freedom and Tenure, Association of American Law Schools," *1954 Proceedings A.A.L.S.* 115, 118; Special Committee of the American Association of University Professors, "Academic Freedom and Tenure in the Quest for National Security," *AAUP Bulletin* 42: 49, 57 (1956); "A Statement of the Committee on Academic Freedom and Tenure Supplementary to the 1956 Report, 'Academic Freedom and Tenure in the Quest for National Security,'" *AAUP Bulletin* 44: 5–10 (1958); Zechariah Chafee, Jr., *The Blessings of Liberty* (1956), 230–231; Harold Taylor, "The Dismissal of Fifth Amendment Professors," *The Annals* 300: 79 (1955); Clark Byse, "Teachers and the Fifth Amendment," *U. of Pa. L. Rev.* 102: 871, 882 (1954).

Chief Justice Parker, recognizes the drastic character of the
dismissal sanction can be expected to give termination criteria a much more limited interpretation than the judge
who views academic freedom as a frill and a luxury. Perhaps the most useful brief statement of the approach which
should govern interpretation of termination criteria is that
of the distinguished student of American freedoms, the late
Professor Zechariah Chafee, Jr., of Harvard University:

[W]hen it comes to cutting short a scholar's career in a
university which promised him life-long security . . . [the]
proceeding resembles a criminal trial and should be similarly
conducted for the purpose of determining the truth of specific
charges against him. These charges should usually be based
upon his personal misconduct in the performance of his
duties. External affairs should normally be considered ir-
relevant unless they involve convictions of serious crimes or
perhaps grave moral delinquencies which unfit him for contact with young men and women. The fact that he holds
unpopular opinions on political matters or associates with
outsiders who hold such opinions is a very dangerous basis
for dismissal, because it opens the way to purges whose scope
can be fixed to meet the passions of the moment and by the
selfish interests of influential groups outside the institution.
Here, as always, the issue ought to be whether this man is
derelict in his duty as a teacher. . . . Dismissal of professors
for new kinds of political and economic heresy is open to
the same objections as the discharge of persons a century ago
for unorthodox religious opinions and the attempted ouster
of E. Benjamin Andrews from the presidency of my own college, Brown, because he was a free-trader and supported
Bryan in 1896.[73]

[73] Foreword to Alan Barth, *The Loyalty of Free Men* (1952),
xxvi–xxvii.

The court which agrees with the Chafee thesis and which therefore believes that causes for discharge should be rigidly limited will be faced with the very important and practical question of what is the proper scope of review of the institution's decision to discharge. May the court make its own independent determination of whether or not the teacher's actions were grounds for dismissal within the meaning of the termination criteria of the tenure plan in question? Or is the court bound by the institution's determination that the teacher's actions satisfied the termination criteria of the plan? Are answers to these questions affected by the fact that the particular plan states that the decision of the governing board shall be final or otherwise purports to reserve conclusive authority to the board?

It is reasonably certain—at least in the absence of a charter provision authorizing discharge at will or of a disclaimer clause in the plan—that the dismissed teacher is not foreclosed from judicial redress solely because the governing board has determined that the plan's termination criteria were satisfied. To uphold a contention that the governing board's decision was binding on the court would be to say that the tenure plan's limitation on the institution's dismissal power expressed only an ideal or a moral commitment of no legal significance. In the absence of a disclaimer clause or a charter provision authorizing discharge at will, it would be unreasonable to interpret the plan as vesting conclusive authority in the governing board.[74]

This is the conclusion that has been reached in cases involving tenure plans of "public" institutions, in which tenure rights often depend more upon sublegislation by the governing board than upon the contract between the

[74] See also note 22 above.

teacher and the institution. Thus in the *Richardson* case discussed above, the rule of the Board of Regents provided, "A staff member under tenure shall be removed only for cause after a hearing before the Board of Regents." The Board of Regents argued that the tenure rule was not binding on it. The Supreme Court of Nevada rejected the contention, holding that the rule had "the force and effect of statute." [75] The board also argued that it was for the board to determine what constituted "cause" within the meaning of the tenure rule. The court again held against the board, stating, "The authorities are overwhelming to the effect that the findings of the investigating board will be reviewed by the courts to determine whether cause for removal has been shown by the evidence." [76]

Although contractual tenure in "private" institutions may for some purposes be distinguished from tenure based on an administrative rule having the "force and effect of statute," the *Richardson* case is persuasive precedent. There the court first decided that the tenure rule had legal significance and then held that the board's determination did not preclude judicial review. The same process of reasoning can be applied to contract tenure. First, do the tenure rules have legal significance, i.e., are they part of the contract between the institution and the teacher? As developed in the preceding section of this chapter, in the absence of a disclaimer clause or a charter provision authorizing discharge at will, the fair inference is that the rules do become part of the contractual relationship.[77] Second, if the court decides that the rules do have legal significance as part of the contract between teacher and institution, it cannot rea-

[75] 70 Nev. 150, 261 P.2d 518.   [76] 70 Nev. 352, 269 P.2d 268.
[77] Page 84 above.

sonably be inferred that the teacher has agreed to accept
the governing board's determination as conclusive, because
the essence of contractual relations is the existence of a
duty for the breach of which judicial redress is available. It
is thus apparent that once it is decided that the teacher had
acquired a contractual right to tenure, the courts are not
foreclosed from reviewing the governing board's determination that grounds for dismissal existed.

The scope or extent of judicial review remains to be
stated. Once again it may be helpful to begin with the case
of a teacher with tenure who is dismissed by a "public" university. When that teacher seeks judicial redress his suit
will be based less upon a theory of breach of contract than
upon the proposition that the governing board's dismissal
action was not authorized by the board's tenure rules,
which have "the force and effect of statute." In legal terms
the argument will be that the board's act was *ultra vires* or
"without or in excess of the board's jurisdiction." In such
a case the court will first determine whether the evidence
adduced at the hearing was sufficient to support the board's
findings of fact concerning the acts allegedly committed
by the teacher; the court will then decide whether "as a
matter of law" the teacher's acts are cause for dismissal
within the meaning of the termination criteria of the institution's tenure rules.[78]

It is true that in the *Richardson* case, the court expressly
acknowledged "full recognition of the right of the regents
to weigh the evidence, to resolve conflicts in such evidence,
to pass upon the credibility of the witnesses, to commit
procedural errors not going to the jurisdiction, and to be

[78] *State ex rel. Richardson* v. *Board of Regents,* 70 Nev. 144, 261
P.2d 515 (1953), 70 Nev. 347, 269 P.2d 265 (1954).

the finders of facts relevant to the issues." [79] Similar language is not lacking in the *Murdock* case.[80] But this disavowal of an independent review should not be taken literally. In both cases the court subjected the charges and the evidence to detailed and critical analysis, and in both cases—but particularly in *Richardson*—it is clear that the court's review was substantially independent.

A similarly independent judicial judgment should be exercised when the propriety of a discharge is presented in an action for breach of tenure-contract against a "private" college or university. Although under generally accepted principles of contract litigation, it might be argued that the "burden of proof" that the discharge was justified must be borne by the institution,[81] reconciliation of the competing interests of the institution and the teacher should not turn on so fine a point. Instead the court should decide in a substantially independent fashion whether the evidence presented at the hearing justifies discharge within the meaning of the termination criteria of the plan in question.[82] Of course, if no hearing has been conducted by the institution, the usual rules of burden of pleading and proof should apply.

Vesting in the courts rather than in governing boards the ultimate power of determining the meaning of the termina-

[79] 70 Nev. 367–368, 269 P.2d 276.

[80] 24 Mass. (7 Pick.) 331–332.

[81] See, e.g., *Scher* v. *School District*, 79 N.D. 818, 830, 59 N.W.2d 805, 811 (1953); Charles B. Labatt, *Master and Servant* (2d ed., 1913), I: 354; A.L.R. Annot. 49: 472, 488 (1927).

[82] This is the approach of the courts in reviewing somewhat analogous decisions of union disciplinary groups. Clyde W. Summers, "Legal Limitations on Union Discipline," *Harv. L. Rev.* 64: 1049, 1084–1086 (1951).

tion criteria obviously decreases the authority of governing
boards in the administration of educational institutions.
This diminution of power of governing boards is necessary
if tenure is to be accorded a full measure of legal significance. Otherwise, the extent and nature of tenure might
depend in considerable part upon the fortuitous factor of
the views of the person or persons who happened to be in
control of the institution. Not many trustees can be expected to take a completely independent and objective position if dismissal proceedings are instituted by the president,
for it must be remembered that the president was appointed
by the trustees and in a very real sense is their representative. If the president, perhaps after consultation with the
chairman or executive committee of the governing board,[83]
alleges that the acts committed by the teacher disqualify
him from continuing as a member of the faculty, it would
not be surprising if most trustees were to conclude that the
president correctly interpreted the termination criteria.[84]
If in turn the reviewing court must defer to the governing
board's interpretation of termination criteria, the tenure
principle could be seriously undermined by a parochial or
prejudiced president. This is not to suggest that presidents
and trustees are evil folk or that judges are paragons of wis-

[83] The authors' experiences with tenure cases over the years support the conclusion that presidents often consult trustee representatives before instituting dismissal proceedings. Sometimes this is
explicitly required by the tenure plan. See, e.g., "The New Constitution" of Augustana College, Art. IV, Sec. 2: "If the President
shall deem the charges sufficiently serious, he shall bring the charges
to the Chairman of the Board."

[84] See, e.g., Russell Kirk's statement of a Regent's remark quoted
in the text, note 65, that "though it was a pity to lose [the accused
professor] Dr. Richardson, it would have been worse to have lost
[the President] Dr. Stout."

dom. It is simply to emphasize that substantially independent judicial review provides an important safeguard against institutional infringement of tenure.

The need for substantially independent judicial review will be diminished in proportion to the extent to which the tenure plan vests final decisional power in termination cases in members of the faculty having tenure and provides for full procedural safeguards. For faculty members having the independent status which tenure assures can bring to bear an objective, expert judgment concerning the teacher's fitness to continue as a member of the family of scholars. A determination so made, whether for or against the teacher, should be accorded a full measure of deference by the courts.

Another facet of the scope of judicial review of a governing board's determination is found in the provisions of some tenure plans which make the decision of the governing board "final" or otherwise conclusive.[85] These provisions

[85] See, e.g., Allegheny College, By-laws, Art. VII, § 8, "The Board of Trustees shall determine the adequacy of the alleged cause and its action thereon shall be final"; Bucknell University, Trustees' Statement of Tenure Principles, § 6, "removal for cause of which the trustees or their duly authorized committee shall be the sole judge"; Augustana College, "The New Constitution," Art. IV, § 2, "a two-third (2/3) vote of the members of the Board shall be the final decision"; Millikin University, Tenure Plans, § 3, "The Board of Managers and the President shall be the judge of conduct and effectiveness"; a Pennsylvania university whose answer requested anonymity, "The decision of the University in the matter of adequate cause or tenure is final"; University of Pennsylvania, Statutes, Art. IX, § 3, "The decision of the executive Board shall be final"; Temple University, Statement of Tenure Policy, "Upon the receipt of [the faculty committee's] report the President or Board of Trustees shall then issue such order as seems fair and just. This order shall be final and conclusive."

are somewhat similar to the disclaimer clauses discussed above. Read literally, the disclaimer clause says the tenure commitment is morally, not contractually, binding; therefore in event of an improper discharge, there can be no legal redress. Read literally, the finality provision says the governing board's decision is the end of the matter—which means, one would suppose, that there can be no redress in event of an improper discharge. Both clauses reflect a distrust or dislike of legal enforcement by a disinterested judiciary, and both seek to retain ultimate power in the hands of the governing board.

Despite their apparent identity of purpose, the two clauses probably would be treated differently by the courts. A likely holding under a disclaimer clause would be that no contractual relations existed.[86] Interpretation of a finality clause would bring into play two related principles of the common law: first, that no man shall be the judge in his own case [87] and, second, that agreements to oust the courts of jurisdiction vested in them will not be enforced.[88] Both

[86] Page 85 above.

[87] Committee on Ministers' Powers, Report, Cmd. No. 4060, at 76 (1932): "The first and most fundamental principle of natural justice is that a man may not be a judge in his own cause." Cf. *Dr. Bonham's Case*, 8 Co. 113b, 118a, 77 Eng. Rep. 646, 652 (1610); *Railway Passenger & Freight Conductors Ass'n. v. Robinson*, 147 Ill. 138, 159–160, 35 N.E. 168, 176 (1893).

[88] *Employee's Benefit Association v. Johns*, 30 Ariz. 609, 619, 620, 249 Pac. 764, 767 (1926): "We are of the opinion that any by-law of an insurance association which provides that in cases of dispute . . . the final and unappealable decisions . . . shall be vested in the association or its officers or business representatives exclusively, is void as against public policy for two reasons: In the first place, because it attempts to oust the courts of the jurisdiction vested in them by the laws of the land to determine controversies . . . ; and second, and even more important, because it also

doctrines reflect the ideal of disinterested judgment, which has deep roots in Anglo-Saxon jurisprudence, and they are sufficient to refute the argument that a finality clause precludes the court from *any* review of the governing board's decision.[89]

The more difficult question remains: To what extent, if any, does a finality clause limit the scope of judicial review of a governing board's dismissal decision? One possible answer is that, since the clause constitutes an attempt to oust the courts of their jurisdiction, it is void, and the rest of the contract will be enforced as though the void provision never existed.[90] A second interpretation would be that the governing board's findings of fact are "final" if supported by evidence, the legal question of whether the facts constituted cause within the meaning of the plan being left to

---

provides in advance that the arbitration or determination shall be left to one of the interested parties to the contract." See also Note, "Exhaustion of Remedies in Private Voluntary Associations," *Yale L.J.* 65: 369, 371 n.13 (1956); A.L.R. Annot. 51: 1420 (1927). For critical comment on the doctrine of "ousting the courts of jurisdiction," see the opinion of Judge Frank in *Kulukundis Shipping Co., S/A,* v. *Amtorg Trading Corp.,* 126 F.2d 978 (C.A.2, 1942).

[89] See remarks of Romer, L. J., in *Lee* v. *Showmen's Guild* (1952) 2 O.B. 329, 353–354, 30 Can. B. Rev. 617, 68 L.O. Rev. 438; *Edwards* v. *Capital Airlines,* 176 F.2d 755 (C.A.D.C.) cert. denied 338 U.S. 885 (1949); *Long* v. *Chronicle Publishing Co.,* 68 Cal. App. 171, 228 Par. 873 (1924); *Patton* v. *Babson Statistical Organization, Inc.,* 259 Mass. 424, 156 N.E. 534 (1927); *Groves* v. *Carolene Products Co.,* 324 Ill. App. 102, 57 N.E.2d 507 (1944), 23 Chi.-Kent L. Rev. 250, 8 U. Det. L.J. 163 (1945). Cf. Dennis Lloyd, "The Disciplinary Powers of Professional Bodies," *Modern L. Rev.* 13: 281, 302–303 (1950)

[90] Consult material cited in note 88 above; see also cases cited in note 89 above.

the court for its substantially independent determination.[91]
A third approach would equate a finality clause to a provision that the governing board may terminate the teacher's
services if it is "satisfied" that cause for determination
exists; in this event, the voluminous precedent concerning
performance to the "satisfaction" of one of the contracting
parties would become applicable.[92] Finally, the clause might
be interpreted to make the governing board's decision final
and conclusive unless proved to be the result of fraud.[93]

[91] It is arguable that this is the interpretation which has been
given to finality provisions in the immigration and selective service
statutes. See discussion in Louis L. Jaffe, "Judicial Review: Question of Fact," *Harv. L. Rev.* 69: 1020, 1047–1050 (1956); "Federal
Habeas Corpus Review of 'Final Administrative Decisions,' " *Col.
L. Rev.* 56: 551 (1956). Cf. *State ex rel. Bourgeois* v. *Board of
Supervisors*, 205 La. 177, 188, 17 So.2d 25, 28 (1944).

[92] *Board of Education* v. *Stotlar*, 95 Ill. App. 250 (1901) (statute
authorized the school board to dismiss a teacher "whenever, from
any cause, the interest of the school may, in their opinion, require
such . . . dismissal"; held, the teacher under this statute "stands
precisely in the position he would have stood in had he made a
contract to teach as long as his services were satisfactory to the
Board of Education"). Cf. *Hartman* v. *Board of Education*, 356
Ill. 577, 191 N.E. 279 (1934); and consult *Independent Life Ins.
Co.* v. *Williamson*, 152 Ky. 818, 154 S.W. 409 (1913); *Chandler,
Gardner & Williams, Inc.* v. *Reynolds*, 250 Mass. 309, 145 N.E.
476 (1924).

For cases interpreting "satisfaction" in employment contracts,
see *Stevens* v. *G. L. Rugo & Sons*, 209 F.2d 135 (C.A. 1, 1953);
Coats v. *General Motors Corp.*, 11 Cal.2d 601, 81 P.2d 906 (1938).

[93] This is the interpretation which the Supreme Court accorded
to a "final and conclusive" clause in a government contract. *United
States* v. *Wunderlich*, 342 U.S. 98 (1951); Congress later enlarged
the scope of review, 68 Stat. 81 (1954), 41 U.S.C., § 321 (Supp. II,
1955). Cf. *Ward* v. *Board of Regents*, 138 Fed. 372 (C.A. 8, 1905)
(statute authorized removal "whenever the interests of the college

Each of these interpretations can be supported by plausible argument and precedent. Which will be adopted when the issue is presented to a court in a tenure case will depend in large part upon (a) whether the court properly assesses the significance of academic freedom and tenure in American higher education and (b) whether the court perceives that dismissal of a teacher with tenure can bring about the same ruinous consequences to the teacher's career that can be caused by disbarment of a lawyer or revocation of a doctor's license.[94] A court which understands the importance of the tenure principle and which recognizes that a teacher dismissed by one institution most likely will not be engaged by another can be expected to adopt the first or second interpretation. The court which has not been enlightened by its own research or by counsel's argument might apply orthodox contract doctrine and conclude that the third or fourth interpretation should be adopted.[95]

---

shall require"; held, court would review only if "fraud or conditions equivalent thereto" existed); A.L.R.2d Annot. 42: 461, 474 (1955).

[94] For elaboration of this thought see the perceptive paper by Edwin O. Stene, "Bases of Academic Tenure," *AAUP Bulletin* 41: 584 (1955); and see *James Murdock, Appellant from a Decree of the Visitors of the Theological Institution in Phillips Academy*, 24 Mass. (7 Pick.) 303 at 331 (1828), quoted above at note 52. Also consult Zechariah Chafee, Jr., "The Internal Affairs of Associations Not for Profit," *Harv. L. Rev.* 43: 993, 1021–1023 (1930); Summers (note 82 above), pp. 1050, 1062.

[95] See *Kalshoven v. Loyola University*, 85 So.2d 34 (La. '56) (contract authorized University to terminate a four-year contract with professor upon six months' notice "because of organizational adjustment or of circumstances *deemed* by the University to be grave" [emphasis supplied]; a personal conflict between professor and Dean developed to a point of "open antagonism" and professor

It is thus apparent that, like disclaimer clauses, finality provisions at best create uncertainty and at worst deprive teachers of full legal protection of the tenure relationship. The remedy for this unhappy situation is obvious—trustee action to delete finality provisions from tenure plans.

A number of the charters studied provide that teachers may be removed for breach of the laws and rules of the institution; [96] occasionally, the letter of notification will state specifically that the appointment is subject to the statutes of the university "as adopted or amended by the Board of Trustees." [97] The legal position of the teacher with tenure under a plan which contains such a provision is not significantly different from that of a teacher with tenure under a plan which does not so provide. For these provisions only make explicit what is implicit in the usual tenure relation-

was discharged pursuant to the contractual provision; held, the decision to discharge was made in "good faith," was not "arbitrary" or "capricious," and the court cannot substitute its "judgment for that of the members of the board of directors . . . whose prerogative it was to make the determination under the provisions of the [contract]").

[96] See note 16 above.

[97] University of Chicago. Compare the following paragraph from the form letter of appointment of Allegheny College; "It is understood that you accept and will abide by such general conditions of constitution and procedure as are stated in the Faculty Handbook or are implicit in the Charter and By-laws of the College and in the catalogue of the College, and by such actions, not necessarily there stated or implicit, as the Trustees, the Faculty or authorities of the College have taken or may take." And consider the penultimate paragraph of the Statute on Tenure of Rockford College: "The foregoing plan may be altered or amended by the Board of Trustees after due notice to the faculty and after giving the faculty an opportunity for conference between committees of the Board and the faculty to consider the proposed amendments or changes."

ship.[98] Governing boards must and do possess authority to make reasonable rules for governance of the institution and its personnel. The rule-making authority must be kept flexible, for changed conditions call for new solutions. Acquiring tenure does not immunize the teacher from reasonable institutional regulation. Whether violation of a rule is ground for discharge should depend on the character of the rule. The drastic nature of the discharge sanction bespeaks the utmost caution in its imposition. An occasional violation of an unimportant rule may be ground for a warning; it is not ground for discharge. This is true whether or not the tenure plan specifically states that violation of rules is ground for discharge.

The rule-making power should not, of course, be permitted to become a subterfuge for defeating the protection which tenure provides. The court should, therefore, be rigorous in its insistence that the rule be reasonable in light of all the circumstances; and one of the circumstances may be the fact that it has a retroactive application to teachers who have earned tenure.[99] It may also be relevant that the trustees have given advance notice of a new policy by promulgating a rule rather than waiting to apply the policy without previous warning in an adjudicative proceeding. Here, as in the case of judicial review of termination cri-

[98] *School City* v. *Sigler*, 219 Ind. 9, 14, 36 N.E.2d 760, 761–763, A.L.R. 136: 1149, 1152–1153 (1941): "In express terms . . . [the contract] contains his agreement to 'observe all rules and regulations of the school authorities.' Without such provision we think this agreement would be read into the contract. The tenure law does not purport to take from the school authorities the management of the schools."

[99] *State ex rel. Keeney* v. *Ayers*, 108 Mont. 547, 92 P.2d 306 (1939).

teria where violation of a rule is not involved, the role of the court is the delicate one of avoiding "both usurpation of . . . [the governing board's] authority and abnegation of judicial responsibility" for protecting the tenure relationship.[100]

PROCEDURE FOR TERMINATION OF TENURE

An essential tenet of the Anglo-American political tradition is that those who exercise governmental power shall not deprive a person of life, liberty, or property without "due process of law." [101] Whatever else due process may connote, it means (with exceptions not here relevant) that notice and hearing must precede final "quasi-judicial" governmental action. Thus, before the state may revoke a professional license, the licensee must be informed of the charges against him and be given an opportunity to be heard.

This enduring insistence upon procedural regularity finds its justification both in conceptions of natural law and in pragmatic considerations. The natural law approach holds the requirement of notice and hearing to be "grounded essentially upon the feeling for fairness which is rooted in man's nature." [102] The pragmatist stresses the importance

[100] See Nathaniel L. Nathanson, "Administrative Discretion in the Interpretation of Statutes," *Vand. L. Rev.* 3: 470, 490 (1950).

[101] See Walter Gellhorn and Clark Byse, *Administrative Law Cases and Comments* (1954), 715–722.

[102] Bernard Schwartz, "Administrative Procedure and Natural Law," *Notre Dame Lawyer* 28: 169, 176 (1953). See also John 7:51, "Doth our law judge any man before it hear him, and know what he doeth?"; Year Book 9 Edw. IV, pl. 15 (1470), "In the law of nature it is required that the parties should be present. . . ."; Fortescue, J., in *The King* v. *The Chancellor of the University of Cambridge,* 1 Strange 557, 567, 93 Eng. Rep. 698, 704 (K.B. 1723),

of enlightened governmental action, urging that notice and hearing should be given in order that the official who is to act may be fully informed concerning the factual bases and probable consequences of the proposed action, and that the person whose interests are to be affected is uniquely qualified to assist in the development and verification of such data. And he argues that, particularly when governmental action or nonaction concerning an individual hinges on controverted facts relating to past events, the methods of a hearing—principally confrontation and cross-examination—will be a superior means for discovering falsehood and correcting unwarranted inferences. The pragmatist would also underscore Justice Jackson's admonition that "due process of law is not for the sole benefit of an accused. It is the best insurance for the Government itself against those blunders which leave lasting stains on a system of justice which are bound to occur on *ex parte* consideration." [103]

Viewed either morally or pragmatically, the teacher with tenure has as great an interest in an opportunity to be heard before dismissal as has the professional licensee before revocation of his license. In each case the harsh sanction of

---

"[E]ven God himself did not pass sentence upon Adam before he was called upon to make his defence. Adam (says God) where art thou? Hast thou not eaten of the tree, whereof I commanded thee that thou shouldest not eat? And the same question was put to Eve also" (quoted in Gellhorn and Byse [note 101 above], pp. 716–717).

[103] Dissenting in *Shaughnessy* v. *United States ex rel. Mezei,* 345 U.S. 206, 224–225 (1953). The Justice says in the same opinion, "Procedural fairness and regularity are of the indispensable essence of liberty. . . . [I]f put to the choice, one might well prefer to live under Soviet substantive law applied in good faith by our common-law procedures than under our substantive law enforced by Soviet procedural practices."

professional disbarment should be imposed only after most careful consideration. In each case that careful consideration can best be achieved by the process of a fair hearing. For a fair hearing gives the affected individual the opportunity—in person or by counsel—to confront his accusers, to introduce evidence on his behalf, to cross-examine witnesses, and to argue before an unbiased tribunal, which will decide on the record so developed whether the prosecution has proved the offenses charged. One cannot be certain, of course, that there are no better means than these of assuring fair and enlightened action when an individual's professional livelihood is at stake. But it can be stated with confidence that if there are other procedures either they have not been discovered or they have not commended themselves to generations of English-speaking judges devoted to the principles of fair play.

But since the due process clauses of federal and state constitutions apply only to government action, there is no constitutional requirement that notice and hearing precede adverse action by nongovernment groups such as corporations, labor unions, professional associations, and "private" educational institutions. Although in some instances this limitation in constitutional protection has been remedied by other legal rules,[104] and although there is emerging a general doctrine that due process protections shall be given to "individuals in their dealings with private groups wielding great economic power," [105] the hard fact remains that in the

[104] Consult Chafee (note 94 above), pp. 1014–1020; Summers (note 82 above), p. 1049; A.L.R.2d Annot. 20: 334, 421, 531 (1951), id. 21: 1397 (1952).

[105] Adolf A. Berle, Jr., "Constitutional Limitations on Corporate Activity—Protection of Personal Rights from Invasion Through Economic Power," U. Pa. L. Rev. 100: 933, 942 (1952). See also

present state of the law there are many areas in which legal guarantees of procedural regularity are lacking.

This defect can be remedied by courts through development of new common-law rules[106] or by legislatures through enactment of statutes requiring compliance with due process requirements[107] or by the parties through con-

---

Adolf A. Berle, Jr., *The 20th Century Capitalist Revolution* (1954), ch. 3.

[106] It is entirely possible that the courts will develop a doctrine that termination of a teacher's employment which reflects on the teacher's reputation or character can only be effected after notice and hearing. See, e.g., *Edinboro Normal School* v. *Cooper*, 150 Pa. 78, 84, 24 Atl. 348 (1892) ("A good character is a necessary part of the equipment of a teacher. Take this away, or blacken it, and the doors of professional employment are practically closed against him. Before this is done there should at least be a hearing, at which the accused may show that the things alleged are not true, or if true are susceptible of an explanation consistent with good morals and his own professional fidelity"); *Murdock* v. *Phillips Academy*, 29 Mass. (12 Pick.) 244, 263 (1831). And consider the relevance of the "association" precedents, note 104 above.

[107] Consider, for example, sec. 15A (b) (9) of the Securities Exchange Act of 1934, 52 Stat. 1071 (1938), 15 U.S.C., § 78o-3(b) (9) (1952), requiring any association of brokers or dealers which seeks registration with the Securities and Exchange Commission to "provide a fair and orderly procedure with respect to the disciplining of members" including specific charges, "opportunity to defend," and a record. Compare statutes forbidding automobile manufactures to cancel dealers' franchises without just cause. E.g., Minn. Stat. Ann., § 168, 27(14)(3), (12) (Supp. 1955), *Willys Motors, Inc.* v. *Northwest Kaiser-Willys, Inc.*, 142 F. Supp. 469 (D. Minn. 1956); R.I. Gen. Laws, c. 2595 Art. VIII, § 2(a) (7, 8), (e) (1950); Wis. Stat., § 218.01(3) (a) (16, 17), (8) (d) (1953), *Kuhl Motor Co.* v. *Ford Motor Co.*, 270 Wis. 488, 71 N.W.2d 420 (1955); see Pub. L. No. 1026, 84th Cong., 2d Sess. (Aug. 8, 1956) (authorizing dealers to sue manufacturers in federal district court for damages from manufacturer's failure to act in good faith in "performing or complying with any of the terms . . . of the

tractual arrangements.[108] But case-law development of new rules often is slow, uncertain, and sporadic. And there is no evidence of imminent legislative action concerning procedural regularity in dismissal proceedings conducted by "private" educational institutions. Indeed, there is good reason to urge that such a development would be unwholesome. For, once a legislature enacts a statutory requirement of a hearing in tenure-termination proceedings, there is a likelihood—or at least a risk—that it would go further and legislate concerning the criteria for termination. All the considerations in favor of the American system of "private" higher education argue against encouraging or permitting legislative intrusion into so sensitive an area. Not only does the experience of the majority of legislators make them less fit than trustees, administrators, and faculty to determine termination criteria but legislatures are more likely than trustees, administrators, and faculty to repress what ought to be free.[109] Thus, at least for the reasonably foreseeable future, reliable procedural protections in dismissal proceedings in private institutions will depend largely on the provisions of the institution's tenure plan.

In the eighty institutions surveyed thirty-one of the seventy-seven which recognize tenure do not expressly provide an opportunity for the teacher to be heard before terminating a tenure appointment. The plans of these in-

---

franchise, or in terminating, cancelling, or not renewing the franchise"); Friedrich Kessler, "Automobile Dealer Franchises: Vertical Integration by Contract," *Yale L.J.* 66: 1135 (1957).

[108] E.g., provisions of collective bargaining contracts requiring disputes to be arbitrated.

[109] The paraphrase is of Judge Learned Hand's statement, "[L]egislatures are more likely than courts to repress what ought to be free." *The Bill of Rights* (1958), 69.

stitutions may state that teachers with tenure will not be dismissed except, e.g., for "adequate cause," but they do not provide for a hearing to determine whether adequate cause exists. Courts have often held that where a statute provides for removal for cause, an opportunity to be heard must precede removal action.[110] Such holdings furnish support for the argument that these tenure plans impliedly require notice and hearing before terminating a tenure appointment, and a court might agree. But there is also the possibility that the court faced with the issue would decide to follow the reasoning of the Supreme Court of Washington interpreting a statute authorizing dismissal of teachers for "sufficient cause":

A teacher is an employee . . . employed in this state by contracts for definite periods with the teacher as one party and the board of directors . . . as the other. In the absence of express legislation we do not think it can be successfully maintained that one party to a contract must sit as a tribunal before exercising its privilege of terminating it.[111]

In this group of institutions, then, it cannot be said with definiteness whether notice and hearing are required. Uncertainty on so vital a matter is a defect which should be corrected by the institutions concerned.

Forty-six of the seventy-seven institutions recognizing tenure expressly provide for a "hearing" (or in one case a "trial") before terminating a tenure appointment. Others state that the teacher shall have the "opportunity to present

[110] E.g., *State ex rel. Howard* v. *Ireland*, 114 Mont. 488, 138 P.2d 569 (1943); *Baird* v. *School Dist.*, 41 Wyo. 451, 287 Pac. 308 (1930); *Clark* v. *Wild Rose Special School Dist.*, 47 N.D. 297, 182 N.W. 307 (1921); see A.L.R. Annot. 99: 336, 354 (1935).

[111] *State ex rel. Board of Directors* v. *Preston*, 120 Wash. 569, 571, 208 Pac. 47 (1922).

his side of the case" or that an "investigation" shall precede termination. Literally interpreted, neither of these latter provisions is an adequate substitute for a hearing. The opportunity to present one's side of the case could be interpreted as requiring only that the teacher could offer rebutting evidence but with no right to cross-examine, or even to know the identity of, his accusers. A provision for an investigation is even more deficient, because all that the requirement of an investigation demands is that the investigator inform himself from whatever sources and by whatever means he deems appropriate.[112] It is basically an ex parte process in which secret evidence may play a major role. As secrecy mounts,

the reliability of the information obtained must necessarily decline. One who is not put to the test of an oath, one who need not face his victim with the charge, one who need not suffer the torment of cross-examination can become quick and reckless with his whispered accusations. The consequences are not only disastrous to the individual; they reflect upon the tribunals which administer the system.[113]

This is not to urge that all the protections of a criminal trial should be made applicable to a proceeding to remove

[112] Although one case has held that a statutory requirement of an investigation by an administrative official should be interpreted to require a hearing, such a holding is not likely in the tenure field. *American Eagle Fire Ins. Co.* v. *Jordan*, 67 F. Supp. 76, (D.C., 1946), rev'd 169 F.2d 281 (C.A.D.C., 1948); cf. *Steen* v. *Board of Civil Service Comm'rs.*, 26 Cal.2d 716, 160 P.2d 816 (1945).

[113] Justice Douglas, Address to American Law Institute, May 20, 1953. Elsewhere Justice Douglas has noted that under cross-examination the stories of secret witnesses "might disappear like bubbles. Their whispered confidence might turn out to be yarns conceived by twisted minds or by people who, though sincere, have poor faculties of observation and memory." *Peters* v. *Hobby*, 349 U.S. 331, 351 (1955) (concurring opinion).

a teacher with tenure. The point is, rather, that when a teacher's reputation, professional stature, and livelihood are at stake, the procedure of an investigation often will not be sufficient to safeguard his interests. Common decency demands that he be given notice and opportunity to be heard in his defense.

Although tenure plans often provide for faculty participation in removal proceedings, the ultimate power of decision usually is vested in the governing board, and typically the plans do not require the board to defer to the faculty decision or recommendation.[114] This retention of final decisional power and lack of provision for accepting faculty judgment probably results from the American tradition—so different from that of European countries—that lay trustees rather than faculty shall govern educational institutions. It may also be based on a belief that retention of final decisional power is a legal necessity. Thus the bylaws of the University of Pittsburgh state:

The power of appointment and the correlative power of removal of an officer of administration or of instruction are by the Charter committed to the Board of Trustees. Any action of the Board which would result in delegating this power to any other body would be *ultra vires*.[115]

Specific clauses in the University's charter provide some, but by no means conclusive, support for the view expressed in the bylaws.[116] In the absence of such specific

[114] A significant exception is the plan of Lincoln University, which makes the decision of the hearing committee final. See above, p. 68.

[115] Ch. 2, Art. II, p. 8, By-laws of the Board of Trustees, University of Pittsburgh.

[116] Section 1, Article IV, of the charter of the University of Pittsburgh states that the majority of the Board of Trustees shall

charter provisions, however, it is highly doubtful that a court would invalidate a tenure plan which gave the faculty a significant, perhaps determinative, responsibility in removal proceedings.[117]

Allocating decisional power between trustees and faculty in the removal process, and indeed in other aspects of college and university government, is a challenging problem of American higher education.[118] Trustee and faculty failure to struggle with the problem—either because it is felt that the law permits only one solution or because tradition offers only one solution—is an unwholesome avoidance of responsibility.[119] Difficult questions call for critical thought and analysis. Neither tradition nor questionable legal as-

be capable of "appointing . . . the professors of the said University . . . and removing them for misconduct." Section 3 of the 1872 Supplement to the Charter states that the Executive Committee shall exercise all the power of the Board of Trustees "except . . . electing a Chancellor or a member of the Faculty." See also *Sittler v. Board of Control*, 333 Mich. 681, 53 N.W.2d 681 (1952).

[117] For general discussion of the delegation problem see Henry W. Ballentine, *Corporations* (rev. ed., 1946), §§ 46–48; William M. Fletcher, *Cyclopedia of the Law of Private Corporations* (rev. ed., 1931), II §§ 494–504; Robert S. Stevens, *Handbook on the Law of Private Corporations* (2d ed., 1949), § 144. Note also that corporations customarily enter into collective bargaining contracts which give final authority to determine "cause" for discharge to an arbitrator. If corporations may vest that power in an arbitrator, it is difficult to see why similar authority may not be delegated to a faculty group. But see *Posin v. State Board of Higher Education*, 86 N.W.2d 31 (N.D. 1957); *Worzella v. Board of Regents*, Sup. Ct. of South Dakota, Dec. 10, 1958.

[118] See discussion in Robert M. MacIver, *Academic Freedom in Our Time*, (1955), chs. 4, 5.

[119] Failure to consider what is *desirable*, as distinguished from what is *legal*, perhaps should not be too severely criticized. For in somewhat related areas of the American scene—procedural regularity and freedom of expression—there is a rather common assumption that governmental action should not be tested on the

sumptions should be permitted to obstruct that rational process. It may also be noted that even if a particular charter provision prohibits delegation of the removal power, the charter can be amended to permit delegation to, or significant participation by, the faculty.

An interesting problem, arising from the allocation of decisional power, is to be found at the University of Pennsylvania; there, the tenure plan vests decisional authority in the Executive Board, and it delegates the equally significant power of deciding whether to initiate dismissal proceedings to the faculty. Article IX of the Statutes of the University states, "The Executive Board, upon the recommendation of a faculty, may suspend or remove . . . any member of such faculty." The person so suspended or removed may secure a hearing upon request. This provision for faculty recommendation is a wholesome expression of the governing board's confidence in the courage, judgment, and integrity of the faculty, as well as an indication of the board's perception that the faculty of which the teacher is a part is in the best position to determine whether reasonable grounds exist for initiating removal proceedings.

The secretary of the University interprets Article IX much more narrowly. In his opinion the Article does not delegate the power to initiate termination proceedings to the faculty, but instead "is merely a statement of the procedure to be followed in any instance where a faculty wished to bring forward for discussion or decision by a Trustee group a case involving possible suspension or removal of . . . [a teacher] within its jurisdiction." [120] The

---

scale of the ultimate social good but rather on the scale of whether the action is constitutional. See Chafee (note 72 above), p. 89.

[120] Communication to the authors dated February 24, 1956.

secretary's opinion runs counter to the understanding of a number of responsible members of the University's faculty, who believe that the stated procedure is exclusive and that therefore a faculty member with tenure may be removed only after his faculty has so recommended. Under the faculty interpretation, the governing board has delegated a significant power to the faculty; under the secretary's interpretation, the board has said only that this is the procedure for faculty initiation of removal proceedings; proceedings initiated by administrative officials or by the governing board will be handled as the board sees fit. As Justice Cardozo said in another context, "The one construction invigorates the . . . [Article]; the other saps its life. A choice between them is not hard." [121]

Whatever may prove to be the correct answer if this problem of construction should reach a court, the situation at the University of Pennsylvania will remain uncertain until the statute is clarified by judicial or trustee action. If the latter course is followed and if the trustees accept the faculty view that the procedure outlined is exclusive, the problem will, of course, be solved. But if the trustees, accepting the secretary's view, should amend the statute to make clear that faculty recommendation is not a condition precedent to removal, uncertainty will continue. For although such a change in the statute plainly would govern future tenure relationships, there is serious question that the change could be made retroactive so as to affect the status of teachers who presently have tenure.[122]

A few tenure plans, instead of making the governing

[121] Dissenting in *Panama Refining Co.* v. *Ryan*, 293 U.S. 388, 439 (1935). See also Edward Potts Cheyney, *History of the University of Pennsylvania* (1940), 367–371.

[122] See text discussion above, p. 116. But cf. *Schulz* v. *Knights of Maccabees of the World*, 236 S.W. 903 (Mo. App. 1922).

board the final decisional authority, vest that power in the president.[123] Giving the president, rather than the trustees, final authority may appear to provide greater protection to the tenure relationship, because college and university presidents usually have risen from the teaching or research ranks and therefore may be presumed to have a more sympathetic understanding of the values of academic freedom and tenure than lay trustees. To be weighed against this presumed superior insight are the following considerations: (a) lay trustees who elect presidents do not always require that their choices be devoted adherents to academic freedom; (b) presidents sometimes appear to be unduly sensitive to public opinion, and too frequently public opinion is found in strident statements of pressure groups rather than in the sober second thought of the community; and (c) judged on the basis of past cases, it may be anticipated that there will be no basic differences between the president and the trustees in most discharge cases.[124] These factors suggest that although giving the president rather than the trustees final authority is a break with the American tradition of trustee control, the change is not one of substance.

Vesting the ultimate decisional power in the president may, however, raise an important question of fairness in the decisional process. In many if not most discharge cases it is the president who (a) decides whether or not to initiate

[123] E.g., Carnegie Institute of Technology. Cf. Bryn Mawr College: A teacher with tenure may be removed "only by the recommendation of the President and the affirmative vote of not less than four members of the Committee on Appointments. . . ." Temple University: "[T]he President or Board of Trustees shall . . . issue such order as seems fair and just . . . [which] order shall be final and conclusive."

[124] See text discussion above, p. 109.

dismissal proceedings, (b) determines which charges shall be pressed, and (c) selects the representative of the institution to prosecute the charges. This degree of involvement in the proceedings may make it difficult if not impossible for the president to exercise an impartial and objective judgment when the case is brought to him for final decision.

Giving the trustees the final decisional power provides for greater separation of the prosecuting and deciding functions. Even here, however, there may still be undesirable predecision involvement by particular trustees—as, for example, in institutions in which the chairman of the governing board either dominates the president or is an equal partner in administration.

One solution to this problem of unwholesome predecision involvement by presidents or trustees is to rely upon the rectitude of these officials. But, to repeat Madison's dictum, "If men were angels, no government would be necessary." Academic government no less than political government must contain safeguards against human frailty. If the tenure plan does not provide the needed safeguards, the courts should remedy the defect by enjoining the prejudiced president or trustee from making or participating in the final decision or by exercising a substantially independent judgment when the dismissal decision is appealed to the courts.[125]

A final observation concerning the importance of procedural regularity in dismissal proceedings may be appropriate. Understandably some readers may be tempted to

[125] See text discussion above, p. 108. See also A.L.R.2d Annot. 20: 344, 378–380, 20: 531, 558–560 (1951), 21: 1397, 1425–1428 (1952); Edwards, (note 2 above), p. 500; Summers, (note 82 above), pp. 1082–1083; *In re Larson*, 17 N.J. Super. 564, 86 A.2d 430 (1952) (concurring opinion).

regard an emphasis upon procedure as an obsession with "legal technicalities." Nothing could be further from the truth. The essence of the American creed is respect for the individual human being, and the ideal that no person shall be deprived of life, liberty, or property without "due process of law" expresses an aspiration which has stirred the minds and hearts of free Englishmen and Americans for centuries.[126] Like most basic concepts the idea of due process of law is not static. It may be lost through desuetude, or it may be refined and developed to meet new threats to basic human rights.

As applied to the individuals who are subject to the rules of academic government, this fundamental principle of human decency requires notice and opportunity to be heard before dismissal. For, as Justice Douglas has so eloquently said, "Who is there who does not cherish his reputation, his professional stature, his honor as much as life itself? What greater inroad on liberty can there be than an official condemnation of a man without due process?"[127] The trustees, administrators, and faculty members who have a sensitive appreciation of the individual's intrinsic importance and essential dignity must therefore insist upon incorporation of due process protections in tenure plans. Responsible institutions in a free society can be satisfied with no less.

[126] For eloquent discussion of the due process ideal, see Erwin N. Griswold, *The Fifth Amendment Today* (1955), ch. 2; John Lord O'Brian, *National Security and Individual Freedom* (1955), 61–62, 74–75; Curtis Bok, "Procedure Comes First," *Publishers' Weekly* 165: 772 (1954).

[127] Address before the American Law Institute, Washington, D.C., May 20, 1953.

IV

Conclusions and Recommendations

TRUSTEES, administrators, and faculties share a common responsibility for integrating the tenure concept with the democratic ideal of intellectual freedom in American higher education. The public at large—including alumni—shares in this responsibility to the extent that it recognizes the importance of the nation's colleges and universities and especially when a tenure case develops into a community problem. The judiciary has a direct responsibility when a tenure case comes to court. It is hoped that the statements which follow will be helpful to each of these responsible interests.

The conclusions and recommendations fall into two groups: (1) specific conclusions and recommendations which apply to the problems considered in chapters II and III, and (2) general conclusions applying to problems resulting from the relationship of tenure to certain institutional characteristics of higher education.

131

SPECIFIC CONCLUSIONS AND
RECOMMENDATIONS

The recommendations that follow do not propose action by state or federal legislative bodies. Nor do they call for the use of outside arbitrators to resolve differences. The prime need is not for extramural intervention, but for each institution of higher learning to engage in systematic discussion and analysis and to take appropriate action to make tenure as positive a force as possible for the good of education. Particularly, trustees, administrators, and faculties should participate in this process in order to reach agreement concerning the proper distribution among them of the powers and responsibilities which relate to matters of tenure. If this basic question can be rightly settled, there will be little need for intercession by outside forces.

The recommendations, which derive from study of a multitude of concrete facts, take the form of generalizations for consideration wherever they may be pertinent. But all generalizations are tentative and subject to correction or replacement in light of new data and fresh analysis. The advantages of diversity and experimentation and the differences in the customs and traditions of the colleges and universities in this country suggest the limitations of any single approach. The proposals thus are not advanced as a uniform code for indiscriminate adoption. They can, however, serve to focus attention on particular issues; and it is hoped they will not be rejected except after careful deliberation.

1. The tenure idea is almost universally recognized; of the institutions here surveyed, all but three state they have conferred tenure on some of their teachers. Since the idea

is so firmly established, the practical need is for further study of the coverage, provisions, and legal significance of various plans and practices.

Recommendation. Because of the values of tenure, outlined in Chapter I, those institutions which have not yet given full recognition to tenure should adopt plans and procedures under which faculty members may achieve tenure. If governing boards and administrators do not inaugurate action, faculty members might appropriately take the initiative, first by local suasion and then, if necessary, by inviting the American Association of University Professors or other organizations to note the institution's failure in this regard. Indeed, professional organizations—such as the Association of American Law Schools and the associations in the subject-matter areas—might well assume a more active role in bringing about sound conditions of tenure in American higher education.

2. Tenure is embodied in a bewildering variety of policies, plans and practices; the range reveals extraordinary differences in generosity, explicitness, and intelligibility. Large or small, public or private, nonsectarian or religiously affiliated, there is no consensus concerning either the criteria or the procedures for acquiring and terminating tenure.

The variety encountered probably results from the differences among the institutions in financial resources, in concepts of educational function, and in particular historical development. This diversity is healthy to the degree that it represents imaginative individuality and reflects the rich variety of free institutions in a democratic society. But it should be harmonized with the characteristics of the teaching profession as a group of experts.

The faculties of American colleges and universities are

made up of men and women whose primary allegiance is to knowledge as a universal value and to teaching as a universal art. Furthermore, teachers are a fairly mobile group and seek appointments in a "national labor market," at least in the years up to the point of achieving tenure. These professional and economic attributes of the teaching group transcend the policies and customs of any particular institution, and teachers are aware of this fact. The college or university which takes a markedly narrow or parochial view of the key idea of tenure is likely to meet frustration or irritation among its faculty, and, on occasion, sharp conflict at the level of a "tenure case." Conversely, the institution which handles tenure in general conformity with the professional status of the persons it appoints will have a more effective faculty and strengthen its power to recruit.

Recommendation. An institution which entertains any doubts about its tenure policy, plan, or practice should examine the whole question; trustees, administrative officials, and the faculty should participate in the process; comparative study should be made of the institution's own handling of tenure and that of other appropriate institutions; and full use should be made of consultative resources of the American Association of University Professors and other groups which have a national perspective.

3. Many institutions, some of unquestioned liberal reputation and tradition, fail to incorporate all of their tenure policy into a written plan. Some that have a fully developed plan choose to leave it in a limbo of unofficial sanction. In those instances where the inadequacy is the result of inertia, there is simply a need for a job to be done. In those in-

134

stances where there is conscious or subconscious antipathy toward the tenure idea, the faculty has an important educational responsibility to perform.

But the absence of a full, written plan may also result from a conviction that custom and tradition, sometimes referred to as the "common law" of academic affairs, are preferable to written regulations. Thus, President Lowell expressed his belief to the Harvard Board of Overseers: "Tradition has great advantages over regulations. It is a more delicate instrument: it accommodates itself to things which are not susceptible of sharp definition: it is more flexible in its application." [1] It has also been urged that written provisions involve an element of inflexibility which is avoided by reliance on custom and tradition. [2]

Unquestionably, an occasional institution may over a long span of years develop a tradition with respect to tenure which is both substantively desirable and clearly defined. At such a college or university sound principles of academic freedom and tenure may obtain despite the absence of an explicit, written tenure plan. But since a happy outcome of this kind has only occasionally been achieved, most institutions would benefit from an attempt to state policy in explicit detail. [3]

Such an endeavor would very likely disclose gaps which need to be filled and, by focusing trustee, administrative, and faculty attention on the problem, would also bring

[1] President A. Lawrence Lowell's report, 1919–1920, quoted by Charles P. Dennison, *Faculty Rights and Obligations* (1955), p. 10.

[2] Dennison (note 1 above), p. 107.

[3] Even the institution governed by a proper tradition may be somewhat handicapped because it cannot be assumed that its tenure policy and practice will be easily perceived by teachers at other places and by the profession at large.

about improvement in tenure policy. A written plan provides a greater degree of legal protection. It also gives faculty members, particularly junior and newer members, information concerning their position. And a written plan guaranteeing academic freedom and tenure rights can be used advantageously to meet attacks by pressure groups in times of stress.[4]

Recommendation. Tenure plans, with possible rare exceptions, should be formally set forth in explicit detail.

4. Legal protection of tenure is insubstantial. Judicial reluctance to decree specific performance of "personal service" contracts, charter provisions authorizing discharge at will, disclaimer and finality clauses, confusing uncertainty in the written plans of some institutions, the complete absence of formal plans in others, the vagueness and inclusiveness of termination criteria, and retention of ultimate decisional authority by most governing boards—all underscore the hazards of reliance on judicial protection of tenure.

Recommendation. Because of the importance of enforcement by an independent judiciary, those institutions with charters and plans containing provisions which hinder legal enforcement should adopt corrective amendments eliminating or clarifying authorizations to discharge at will, dis-

[4] "If a professor, for example, were propounding unpopular views and causing an irresponsible minority in the community to demand his dismissal, a legal commitment regarding the professor's rights and obligations might be a more effective defense of the college's action than an effort to present the merits of the case to an excited public." Dennison (note 1 above), p. 103. Pages 101–118 of the Dennison book contain an excellent discussion of the general problem "Written Commitments vs. Less Formal Understandings" in academic government.

claimer clauses, finality provisions, confusing ambiguities, and vague termination criteria which only remotely bear upon a faculty member's fitness to teach, to engage in research, or to associate with students.

5. The role of the courts in reviewing dismissal determinations by institutions which have sound, written tenure plans should be quite conventional and relatively simple. It would be the court's responsibility to determine whether the requirements of the plan had been complied with. Was there failure to follow the stated procedure? Were the facts proved by a preponderance of the evidence? Did the proved facts constitute disqualifying conduct within the meaning of the plan?

Courts reviewing dismissal determinations made under plans which did not conform to sound principles would have a more difficult task. For if the institution had not accorded the faculty member academic due process or if it had discharged the faculty member for reasons other than professional unfitness, the tenure principle would have been infringed and academic freedom undermined. But traditional doctrine would say that in the absence of a contractual limitation on the institution's power of appointment and termination, the faculty member in a private institution, at least, had no legally protectible interest. The answer to this argument is that, as important as it is, the social interest in freedom of contract may in some instances be subordinated to a more important social interest—academic freedom.

Recommendation. The creative judge, recognizing the vital importance of academic freedom in our society and its customary acknowledgment in long-established usage, should feel free to hold that in the absence of a specific disclaimer or finality clause, the faculty member of long service has acquired a *status* and that an incident of this status is protection from discharge except for good cause and after proceedings which comply with the principles of academic due process.[5] The remedy for infringement of tenure should include an order of reinstatement.

6. All faculty members, particularly those having tenure, should recognize that membership in the community of scholars of American higher education entails particular obligations. Foremost and best recognized is conscientious discharge of research, teaching, and assigned administrative responsibilities. In addition, the faculty member must remember that as "a man of learning and an educational officer . . . the public may judge his profession and his institution by his utterances. Hence he should at all times be accurate, should exercise appropriate restraint, should show respect for the opinion of others, and should make every effort to indicate that he is not an institutional spokesman." [6] He should be scrupulous in giving reasonable advance notice of an intention to resign, for the process of replacing faculty members, especially those with tenure, is time-consuming and difficult.

Recommendation. The obligation to discharge one's primary responsibilities with fidelity and diligence, to give advance notice of intention to resign, to act with restraint, to show respect for the opinions of others, and to avoid

[5] See materials cited in Chapter III, notes 104–106. Consult also the provocative essay by Professor Thomas A. Cowan, "Interference with Academic Freedom: The Pre-Natal History of a Tort," *Wayne L. Rev.* 4: 205 (1958).

[6] 1940 "Statement of Principles," *AAUP Bulletin* 44: 291 (1958).

giving the impression of being an institutional spokesman should be recognized by faculty members. Faculty groups, such as the American Association of University Professors, might appropriately assume a greater initiative in this respect than has been customary in the past.

7. Religious freedom is one of the preferred American freedoms. It accounts for the hospitable reception accorded sectarian colleges and universities by our society. But sectarian colleges and universities are nonetheless educational institutions; and as such they must recognize the legitimate demands of academic freedom and tenure.

Recommendation. The principles of academic freedom and tenure here recommended should be applicable to educational institutions conducted by religious groups, with the proviso that reasonable limitations because of the religious objective of the institution may be imposed by agreement entered into between the institution and the faculty member at the time of his appointment.[7]

8. Some institutions, particularly those which grant tenure on an *ad hoc* basis, object to the "automatic" provision of some tenure plans. This objection is based on a misapprehension. The only automatic element in these plans is the fixing of the date at which an institution must distinguish between its hitherto unrestricted right not to ap-

---

[7] The precise character of the "reasonable limitations" presents an extremely difficult problem, which deserves further study. For opposing viewpoints on the general subject of academic freedom and the denominational university, see Robert M. MacIver, *Academic Freedom in Our Time* (1955), 285–289; Journet Kahn, "The Threat to Academic Freedom," *Proceedings of the American Catholic Philosophical Association* 30: 160 (1956).

point and its now imminent obligation. A college or university is privileged, under the standards of the profession, to release with adequate notice any teacher in any rank during his probationary period. But once that period has been served and it is decided that a teacher shall be retained, privilege should yield to obligation. Refusal to grant tenure to a teacher who has served his probation and is reappointed constitutes failure on the part of the institution fully to confirm its judgment. Such a failure is unjust to the teacher and harmful to institutional morale.

Recommendation. Tenure plans should provide that retention of a teacher beyond a stated probationary term confers tenure.

9. A teacher who has completed his professional training, served at an institution for something like seven years, and has been reappointed is in some institutions required further to qualify for tenure by achieving a particular rank. The difficulty with this criterion is that promotion is often conditioned by the financial and actuarial picture in an institution.[8] As for the argument that an all-rank tenure plan is conducive to an all-tenure staff, it fails to recognize that any rank or any post can be kept fluid by not retaining personnel beyond the probationary period.

Recommendation. Tenure plans should be of the all-rank

[8] [George Pope Shannon], "The 1940 Statement of Principles does not associate tenure with rank, nor is it morally defensible that a man or woman of proved competence should have to wait for tenure on the happy accident of death in the superior ranks. Security of tenure and opportunity for promotion are two different things and their confusion has been and is the cause of much injustice." "Editor's Notes," *AAUP Bulletin* 42: 585 (1956).

type; achievement of rank should not be a condition of tenure.

10. A few institutions go no further than to state that tenure must or may be "considered" after a specified probationary period. Such a provision does not constitute a tenure plan. A loose commitment of this kind, happily often stronger in practice than in promise, is an unnecessary aberration from general tenure principle, harmful to staff morale and a handicap upon recruiting.

Recommendation. Provisions requiring consideration of tenure at the conclusion of the probationary period should be replaced by provisions requiring the granting of tenure.

11. Tenure is based in part on retention; retention is based in part on the meeting of evaluative standards. Yet only thirty-eight of the institutions surveyed state the grounds upon which teachers are judged for promotion and tenure, and some of these statements are inadequate.

Recommendation. The best practices with regard to standards for acquisition of tenure should be studied and generally embodied with appropriate local modifications.

12. Only twenty-six of the eighty institutions studied provide for faculty action on recommendations for tenure. Thus only one-third of these colleges and universities require responsible action by the best-informed group on the most important kind of personnel decision made on the campus. Under these circumstances the teaching profession is not likely to feel that acquisition of tenure is governed by genuinely professional standards; nor will trustees and

administrators benefit by the considered and official advice
of the experts who do the institution's work.

Recommendation. Tenure plans should provide for official action by the faculty, at one or more levels, on all
decisions about acquisition of tenure.

13. Only thirty-five of the institutions offer procedure
governing appeal from denial of tenure, and of this group
of thirty-five only thirteen permit such an appeal to an all-
faculty group. This means that 84 per cent of these institutions have not provided procedures whereby a faculty
member who believes himself unjustly or wrongly denied
tenure may obtain a judgment by his peers. This situation
demeans the teaching profession.

Recommendation. Provision should be made for appeal
from denial of tenure which at some stage permits judgment
by a standing committee of the faculty.

14. Once a faculty member has acquired tenure, his appointment should be terminated only for professional unfitness or perhaps because of financial exigencies. The
standard for dismissal because of actions within the academic institution should be incompetence in teaching or
research or gross personal misconduct which unfits the
faculty member for association with students. External
affairs only become relevant if they involve "grave moral
delinquencies which unfit him for contact with young men
and women." [9] As President Conant stated in his final annual
report to the Board of Overseers of Harvard University:

[9] Zechariah Chafee, Jr., Foreword to Alan Barth, *The Loyalty of
Free Men* (1952), xxvi.

142

If the trustees or administrative officers of a university were to engage in any investigation of a professor's activities as a citizen, the life of the university would be destroyed. Of that I am sure. Outside of his classroom a professor speaks and acts as a private citizen. What his views may be or how wisely or foolishly he speaks is no concern of the university administration, provided he is not acting illegally as determined by due process of law.[10]

Dismissing a faculty member for external actions is an extremely delicate process involving unusual hazards. For the temptation is to base such a decision on the adjudicator's moral code rather than upon the more explicit standard of illegal conduct. Yet to remove a faculty member with tenure because he exercised a choice within the law is to open the way for discharges for other lawful actions, because purges once begun often know no stopping place. This is not to imply that discharge is appropriate in every instance in which a faculty member has violated the law. It is only when the violation involves a serious criminal offense that the extreme sanction of banishment from the teaching profession is appropriate. Here the counsel of Judge Charles E. Wyzanski, Jr., one of the nation's most distinguished judges and then-President of the Board of Overseers of Harvard University, deserves emphasis:

A University is the historical consequence of the mediaeval *studium generale*—a self-generated guild of students or of masters accepting as grounds for entrance and dismissal only criteria relevant to the performance of scholarly duties. The men who become full members of the faculty are not in substance our employees. They are not our agents. They are

[10] President James Bryant Conant's report, 1951–1952, p. 21.

143

not our representatives. They are a fellowship of independent scholars answerable to us only for academic integrity.

We undertake the responsibility for handling infractions of university codes occurring within the times and places where our certificate operates. On these matters we possess the best available evidence, we have familiar canons to apply, and we have established processes of judgment and punishment.

What faculty members do outside their posts, we should leave to outside authority. . . .

[A university] is not and must not become an aggregation of like-minded people all behaving according to approved convention. It is the temple of the open-minded. And so long as in his instruction, his scholarship, his relations with his associates and juniors a teacher maintains candor, and truth as *he* sees it, he may not be required to pass any other test.[11]

Recommendation. The standard for dismissal of a faculty member with tenure should be incompetence in teaching or research or gross personal misconduct which unfits the faculty member for association with students.

15. Neither specially qualified personnel nor due process procedures may be needed to ascertain simple facts pertaining to narrowly defined problems of relative unimportance. But when factual issues relate to a particular area of knowledge, when the decisional body is vested with great discretion in interpreting and applying the standards of decision, and when the ultimate decision will directly affect an individual's reputation and livelihood, the constituency of the decisional body and the procedures it fol-

[11] Charles E. Wyzanski, Jr., "Sentinels and Stewards," *Harvard Alumni Bulletin*, Jan. 23, 1954, p. 316.

lows in reaching its decision are of the greatest consequence. This, of course, is the situation in tenure dismissal proceedings. The adverse effects of a dismissal on the individual's career are extremely grave. The ultimate issues of incompetence or misconduct which unfits the faculty member for association with students can best be resolved by individuals whose training and experience gives them the insight needed to make these determinations intelligently and whose professional status is sufficiently secure to make it likely that they will apply objective standards of judgment, unaffected by political or public relations pressures.

Notwithstanding the vital importance of fair procedure and of faculty participation in proceedings to terminate a tenure appointment, the provisions in most tenure plans dealing with these matters are rudimentary in character. Perhaps this is an area in which custom and tradition are more significant than formal structure. Wholesale revision of plans which have proved their merit in actual operation would certainly be unwise. But in the absence of a demonstrated effective tradition, there is need in most institutions for careful delineation of procedural rights and of the role of the faculty in dismissal proceedings.

Once attention has been focused on the procedure problem, it should not be difficult to reach general agreement concerning minimal procedural safeguards. For legal due process is a generally accepted ideal, and it has a hard core of content that can readily be incorporated into academic due process.

More difficult will be the problem of allocating decisional responsibility among the trustees, the administration, and the faculty. For nearly forty years the American Association of University Professors through its Committee on the

Place and Function of Faculties in Colleges and University Government has wrestled with the general problem.[12] Although the Committee has noted progress in some respects, the fact remains that there is no consensus concerning either the constituency of the hearing group or the extent of faculty participation in the decisional process. Whatever the merits of faculty participation in other areas of academic government, the faculty should have the primary responsibility to determine who shall be appointed to the faculty and who shall be removed therefrom. The reasoning underlying this conclusion is that governing boards, "being composed for the most part of busy men of affairs," [13] do not have the time and probably do not have the competence to reach carefully considered, fully informed judgments concerning academic personnel.

It is particularly important that the faculty be given primary responsibility in dismissal cases. The president usually is the one who initiates and supervises presentation of the charges against the faculty member; therefore he should be disqualified from adjudicating the case—although he is quite free to state his opinion as the chief administrative officer. Not only do the trustees as a rule not possess any particular competence to judge a faculty member's professional fitness, but their usual reliance on, and deference to, the president's advice [14] tends to make his dis-

[12] See "Report of Committee on the Place and Function of Faculties in College and University Government," *AAUP Bulletin* 39: 300 (1953); 41: 62 (1955).

[13] Report of Committee on the Place and Function of Faculties in College and University Government, 1920, quoted in *AAUP Bulletin* 39: 301 (1953).

[14] *Ibid.*, 301–302: "Boards of trustees, being composed for the most part of busy men of affairs frequently possessing no special com-

qualification their own. In any event, they are less impartial judges and less qualified to reach intelligent decisions concerning matters of professional fitness than experienced members of the faculty. The senior faculty members with tenure do more than anything or anyone else to determine the quality, character, and strength of the institution. They have devoted years of service to the institution, and they have an abiding interest in its welfare. They, rather than busy lay trustees, have the ability, experience, and time to reach fair and informed judgments concerning professional fitness.

Recommendation. Institutions should revise their tenure plans so as (1) to provide for adequate due process protection in dismissal proceedings and (2) to vest in the faculty or its elected representatives primary responsibility for deciding whether the accused faculty member is professionally unfit. In making this revision, consideration might appropriately be given to the following suggestions:

a. Proceedings to dismiss a teacher with tenure should be initiated by the cognizant administrative official only after he has made sufficient investigation to determine that reasonable grounds exist for the belief that the faculty member has committed acts justifying dismissal. In making this determination, the administrative official should have the assistance of an elected faculty advisory committee. In the

---

petence to pass judgment on matters of educational policy rely chiefly upon the president for information and advice as to how things are going and what things should be done. . . . Thus, the powers actually exercised by university presidents are, to a very great extent, not powers legally conferred upon the office by charters, but exercised by the incumbent of the office as surrogates for groups of busy men who are not educational experts, and, fortunately, in most cases know that they are not."

usual course of events both the administrative official and the faculty advisory committee would interview the faculty member, and opportunity for informal adjustment would be afforded.

b. In event of failure to adjust the matter informally, written charges should be served on the faculty member by the administrative official. The charges should be set forth in as much detail as is practicable; they should be accompanied by a summary of the evidence on which the charges are based and a list of witnesses to be called. The time and place of the hearing should be specified. The faculty member should also be furnished copies of relevant documents —charter, statutes, and rulings by the governing board, administrative officials, and faculty. The faculty member should reply in writing to the charges.

c. The hearing on the charges should be held before a standing committee of [five] faculty members with tenure elected by the faculty. The members of the hearing committee should be individuals of known independence and objectivity who can be expected to exercise an informed judgment concerning the teaching and research qualifications of the class of faculty members to which their jurisdiction extends. In smaller colleges this goal might be achieved by electing the members from the entire faculty; in larger universities, a separate hearing group might appropriately be elected by the faculty of each school. The committee should elect one of its members as chairman.

d. The hearing committee may be able to decide the case in favor of the faculty member on the basis of the charges made and the answers thereto. If not, the hearing should be conducted at a place and time fixed by the hearing committee. The hearing should be private unless the faculty member requests otherwise. A record of the hearing should be kept by a stenographer furnished by the institution. The administrative official should have the burden of proving the charges by a preponderance of the evidence. The hearing should comply with the requirements of academic due process, including the assistance of an adviser or counsel for both the faculty member and the administrative official, confrontation, cross-examination of witnesses, assistance of the institution in securing witnesses, opportunity to submit oral and written argument, and a decision on the record by the hearing group. The hearing group should decide the matter as promptly as possible and furnish a transcript of the record and copies of its written findings, reasons, and conclusions to the administrative official and faculty member.

e. Unless there is a defect of procedure, or a failure to prove the charges by a preponderance of the evidence, or a misinterpretation of the applicable termination criteria, the decision of the hearing committee should be final. On appeal by the faculty member, the governing board should determine whether there has been a defect of procedure, or failure to prove the charges by a preponderance of the evidence, or a misinterpretation of termination criteria. In event of such appeal, both the faculty member and the administrative official should have the right to appear before the governing board and to submit oral and written argument. The governing board should decide the case on the basis of the hearing committee's report and the record of the hearing and should also prepare written findings, reasons, and conclusions which should be given to the administrative official and faculty member.

f. Neither the faculty member nor the cognizant administrative official (or his superior) should directly or indirectly discuss the case with, or in any way attempt to influence, any member of the hearing committee or of the governing board. Both the faculty member and the cognizant administrative official should be permitted to move to disqualify any prejudiced member of the hearing committee or of the governing board. Such motion should be decided on the record by the remaining members of the committee or board. The faculty member and administrative official may agree that the remaining members of the committee shall adjudicate the case or that they shall have authority to co-opt a qualified substitute for the disqualified member; in event of failure so to agree, a new member should be selected by the same process as was employed in choosing the disqualified member.

g. Suspension during the proceedings should occur only in the rare case where there are compelling reasons for the belief not only that the faculty member has committed disqualifying acts but also that they are of a character which would seriously prejudice his teaching or research pending final decision.

THE RELATIONSHIP OF TENURE TO CERTAIN INSTITUTIONAL CHARACTERISTICS OF HIGHER EDUCATION

The institutional characteristics of American higher education reveal an accommodation between those major forces which shape the national social structure and the more particular, often nonnational traditions which have grown out of the performance of a long-established special function. In many ways the accommodation has been successful; by and large, social forces and academic traditions have interacted to produce a respectable number of colleges and universities noted for productive scholarship. Nevertheless, recurrent friction and occasional open dispute indicate that some aspects of these places of learning are less than fully harmonious. Four problems are of immediate importance for the tenure principle.

The Problem of Disparate Values

Some trustees differ from some teachers in their view of the function of education. The difference appears to result from the fact that these trustees and teachers are governed by fundamentally disparate values. This problem should be frankly explored in the hope of greater harmony and for the good of tenure.

From the beginning, the trustees of American institutions of higher education have been the representatives of one or another major social power, often the dominant one.[15] In the earliest period this power was usually that of the dominant church in the community, and this is still true of a number of private, religiously-oriented institutions. Later, and now preponderantly, the controlling power is the whole complex of forces that seek to conserve the existing social structure. Proof is to be found in the populating of boards of trustees by administrators of financial accretion, business lawyers, churchmen, and persons who have held responsible positions in government. Significantly, among the groups who make important contributions to human welfare but receive only minimum representation on educational governing boards are teachers.

[15] Richard Hofstadter and Walter P. Metzger, *The Development of Academic Freedom in the United States* (1955).

Governing boards of colleges and universities have unquestionably often shown remarkable understanding and imagination in managing their institutions. Nevertheless, they have at other times lacked the degree or kind of experience necessary for expert authority over an academic enterprise. For example, there were once frequent instances where a majority of a board of trustees sided with those elements in the community who had ignorantly disapproved of certain explorations of subject matter or of some pedagogical practice. Such cases still occasionally arise. Now, more often, the failure is of the sort where the governing board aligns itself with community disapproval of a teacher's free expression or action as a citizen. In all these matters, the mistake of the governing board appears to derive from too great devotion to the value system of conservation and a limited perception of the essential academic needs of exploration and freedom.

The values which command the devotion of teachers are distinctly different. The scholar's primary allegiance is to free inquiry; he feeds upon its fruits, he is committed to its practices, he hopes that it will justify his labor. In the practice of this freedom, the teacher cannot remain a scholar if he pays much attention to whether society regards his exploration and his results as mainly supportive of the existing scheme of things, or mainly useful to some plan for radical change. Of course he knows that he may sometimes be labeled a "revolutionary," at other times a "reactionary," and perhaps both simultaneously if he takes the middle ground at a time of sharp division of public opinion. But he must take that risk, because otherwise he would find himself rejecting the intellectual discipline of scholarship and the fundamental value of his profession—the quest for a better truth.

Satisfactory practical reconciliations between the disparate values of trustees and teachers are sometimes achieved. A college or university may over a period of time develop a tradition of such scholarly splendor that all concerned will live happily together under its beneficent control. A governing board, as has been noted, may be made up of individuals who understand and strongly support freedom of inquiry. Most often, probably, a satisfactory environment for scholarship is achieved by the wisdom of an expert president as he goes about his daily task of integrating the demands of society and the principles of the academic tradition. Unfortunately, the accidents of time and the strains of life can—with rather shattering unexpectedness—disturb any of these adjustments. The tensions of hot and cold war, the agonies of institutional poverty, conflict over racial integration—all of these have produced crises where the established order demands a safe conservation or even an unquestioning conformity. No teacher who is a scholar will fail to resist such pressures; he must with proper decorum assert his permanent commitment to the quite different values of academic freedom, even if his teaching appointment is thereby endangered.

The implications for tenure of any conflict between the general social principle of conservation and the particular academic principle of freedom are obvious. If the issue is to be wisely debated between the governing board and the faculty, the teachers who make up the faculty must have security—i.e., proper standards and procedures governing acquisition and termination of tenure. If these safeguards exist, there is a chance that disparity can be transcended for the good of all. If the protections are not present, it is likely that the weaker party will suffer by the fact that it has been drawn into controversy; the teacher will lose his job and the institution and the community will lose their chance to understand better the nature of the educational function.

It may be significant that no college or university offers criteria or procedures by which the faculty—the persons whose lives and welfare are one with that of the institution —can take action to remove a trustee of demonstrated incompetence.

The Problem of the Employer-Employee Relationship

The status of a teacher in American higher education sometimes receives different interpretations and emphases by the governing board and by the teacher, often most seriously different in tenure disputes.

To begin with, the teacher is aware of the fact that the first great universities—Bologna, Padua, Heidelberg, Paris, Oxford, and Cambridge—consisted, corporately, of the faculty. This was true when they began their work and, despite the passing of centuries, it remains largely unchanged. And the contributions to learning of these archetypes, and of other European institutions modeled upon them, have been of the highest order. In America, on the other hand, the early colleges were established and given their original support chiefly as service institutions; they were usually charged directly with such tasks as the preparation of the clergy or the imparting of culture to the sons of the gentry. Only slowly and late did the idea emerge of the independent pursuit of knowledge under the control of the faculty. But by now it is clear that the concept of a "community of scholars" is gaining increasing acceptance in this country. Although faculties do not seek "ownership" and identification as the legal corporate entity, they are more and more coming to regard themselves as the central reality of their institutions. Faculties whose duty is to carry on the educational process are increasingly inclined to seek the authority needed for the effective discharge of that responsibility.

Thus both the historical origin of higher academic institutions and the present developing awareness of a need for greater power, which has been very largely granted in some of this country's most distinguished institutions, lead the teaching profession to reject the idea of simple employment as correctly expressive of the relationship between the teacher and the college or university.

Many trustees bring to their work a different point of view. Most members of governing boards are probably, in their main occupation, either employers or engaged in the service of employer interests. Hiring and firing is part of the ordinary business of life. And when an individual first becomes a member of a governing board he meets a situation which does not seem very different; on the campus, too, persons are engaged for specific terms at specific salaries. The ordinary apparatus of payrolls, withholdings, and other routine processes apply to teachers as they customarily apply to employees. Also, the trustee may find in the charter of his institution a stated authority to engage and dismiss the teaching staff, without any contiguous qualification of that power.

In this normative scheme of things, the trustee then discovers the complicating principle of tenure, which may be embodied in a formally adopted set of rules governing standards and procedures. If he seeks an explanation, he learns about the need for co-ordinate measures of responsibility and authority and about the compelling social necessity for protection of the teacher's freedom. Obviously insistence upon the classical concept of an employer-employee relationship does not furnish a proper base for resolving a dispute in this area between the board and the faculty. And so, with more or less illumination and good will, the trustee addresses himself to a review of the teacher's position in the academic complex. The range, variety, and success of that review in eighty institutions is indicated by the detailed findings of this study.

Leaving aside the particular achievements or failures in establishing tenure on a sound basis, one general conclusion seems clearly established. Review of the tenure situation in any institution should continue until all permanent members of the faculty are fully recognized as essential elements of the authority of the corporation in matters relating to the acquisition or termination of permanent status.

The Problem of the Teacher as an Expert

A teacher in a college or university has received social recognition as an expert in his subject and in the practice of teaching. This means that he should receive the special freedoms and defenses which society normally accords to experts, because so much effort has been invested in their training and because they are so difficult to replace. A judge, for example, is given a high degree of personal freedom and security by superior rewards and long tenure of office—because he discharges the august responsibility of administering justice. Likewise, the surgeon, although unprotected by investiture, receives by community agreement an extraordinary status—because of his overwhelmingly vital function. The teacher regards himself as carrying on work of no lesser importance—his charge as an expert is safeguarding the life of reason. Of course, judge, surgeon, and teacher, as men, derive some private benefit from the privilege attached to their expert status, but that good fortune is coincidental. The social principle remains unchanged: the welfare of society requires that valuable servants be free and safe to do their work.

It is a commonplace of history that society often turns against its leaders, including its experts, when things go seriously wrong. Whether the fault is in the judgment of the expert or in the resources and authority put at his disposal is not always carefully looked into. This principle of blame operates in the United States as it does elsewhere and apparently with more than average speed when the expert works in the realm of ideas. The obscurantism which marked the McCarthy era was not the first in American history.

Teachers, most of whom are professionally concerned with ideas, know that social disapproval is likely at some time or other to harass most practicing experts. They therefore propose to protect themselves as well as they can by institutionalizing the standards and procedures which determine their status. Hence the tenure principle; hence, most importantly, judgment by other teachers within a tenure system.

The General Problem of Freedom in Academic Institutions

Important as tenure is, it is but one aid in the never-ending task of creating and maintaining the freedom which fosters creative scholarship in American higher education. There are other dangers to academic freedom than those which tenure protects against.[16] Foremost among these is the unwillingness or inability of some administrators to give ungrudging acceptance to the spirit of tolerance and equality which is part of the philosophy of academic freedom. In institutions where this attitude prevails, the existence of a formal or informal tenure plan is no assurance that academic freedom is recognized in any meaningful sense.

Fortunately, it is not likely that many administrators would agree with the following statement made by a president of one of the institutions studied: "The administration of the college is opposed to tenure as a policy. . . . No teacher should want to remain where he is not wanted. Most administrations can and do circumvent the finest tenure provisions by encouraging resignations." The statement has the merit of frankness, but it is fatally defective in its perception. There is no recognition of the cardinal principle that those who determine unwantedness must be qualified to render such a judgment and must act according to standards which are appropriate and according to procedures which are just.

Unfortunately, and more significantly, there is evidence that academic freedom, and tenure along with it, is sometimes endangered by the failure on the part of an administrator to maintain a general spirit of freedom in his relations with his faculty. Thus, a teacher at one of the institutions surveyed wrote as follows:

[16] See Lawrence Podell, "Assault from Within," *The Commonweal* 65: 427 (1957), critically appraising "four influences" which have caused a decline in academic responsibility. Professor Podell also notes that academic freedom is rarely infringed by the "dynamic dismissal of a professor. Often, less noticed, but more effective limitations are accomplished through the altering of employment practices, standards, budgets, salaries and curricula. . . ."

I am sure you will agree that the "health" of the relations between administration and faculty as a whole directly bears on whether tenure at an institution is in good, bad, or indifferent health. I am going to say to you exactly what I think by way of general comment on this score. . . . I find academic freedom here . . . in a state of indifferent health. Formal discussions in faculty meetings and in committee meetings do not seem to me pervaded by a spirit of free discussion, undertaken in the belief that decisions of importance are really being shaped in those meetings. Decisions of importance are largely being formed by the president; and to the extent that faculty are consulted in forming them, they are consulted on the whole in an *ad hoc* manner. A good many of the faculty seem to feel the futility of attempting to say what they really think, on what they think of real importance, by the time matters come up for open discussion between faculty and administration. Our president is a man of ability, an ambitious man, much preoccupied with the promotion of the college and its problems of finance. Yet he tends to hold the reins of decision on matters of mutual concern to himself and the faculty rather tightly within his own hands. In short, his administration is more autocratically disposed than otherwise. Where this remains the case, an uneasiness obtains in matters of appointment and tenure, in spite of reassuring progress that has been made in stated policy.[17]

[17] The views of this writer should be compared with those expressed by a faculty member at another institution: "No clear statutory definition of tenure for the various ranks exists in written form. . . . In actual practice, however, department heads, deans, and other administrators have shown that they are acquainted with and respect fully the AAUP principles of tenure. . . . In the opinion of the executive committee of the . . . [AAUP] Chapter, the conditions of academic freedom at . . . may be characterized as very good."

There is, unhappily, no readily available corrective for this situation. As Burke said, "Constitute government how you please, infinitely the greater part of it must depend on . . . the prudence and uprightness of ministers of state." [18] And so in the case of academic government, endeavors to improve formal structures must not be permitted to obscure the importance of efforts to seek out trustees, administrators, and faculty members of wisdom, courage, and rectitude.

The present scene in American higher education is one of general peace except for re-evaluation of the situation created by the recent "security" hysteria. The economy of education is not very rewarding to the individual, but he is not in acute distress and is at least receiving attention.

And yet the picture is far from satisfactory. If a period of major strain should arrive, there is strong likelihood that the latent, unresolved differences between the trustee attitude and the faculty attitude would again produce a series of harmful controversies. The conflict between the employment and tenure principles of staff appointment would recur. The teaching profession would again need to wield defensive weapons, which, although it might be temporarily successful, would have the unfortunate consequence of taking teachers away from their main business.

This point in time is perhaps as appropriate as any for serious, unimpassioned effort to improve the structure of higher education. The purpose of this study has been to suggest that one promising avenue toward productive reconstruction is that of improving the policies, plans, and practices which implement the tenure principle.

[18] *Thoughts on the Cause of the Present Discontents,* in *Works* (1826), I: 379.

Appendices

THE eighty colleges and universities selected for study are listed in Appendix A. The questionnaire sent those institutions is reproduced in Appendix B. Appendices C, D, E, and F reproduce four important documents evolved by organizations which have a particular concern with the standards and procedures of acquisition and termination of tenure and with academic due process.

A

List of Institutions Studied

Name and location	Charter	Teaching staff*			Students †
		Total	Full-time	Tenure	
The Academy of the New Church, Bryn Athyn, Pa.	1877	32	26	25	58
Albright College, Reading, Pa.	1856	47	39	23	523
Allegheny College, Meadville, Pa.	1817	81	70	43	939
Augustana College, Rock Island, Ill.	1865	74	61	29	1,134
Augustana Theological Seminary, Rock Island, Ill.	1860	12	11	10	187
Beaver College, Jenkintown, Pa.	1853	55	*not stated*		486
Blackburn College, Carlinville, Ill.	1869	30	29	16	331
Bradley University, Peoria, Ill.	1897	174	132	95	2,297
Bryn Mawr College, Bryn Mawr, Pa.	1885	117	81	41	748
Bucknell University, Lewisburg, Pa.	1846	137	136	52	1,868
California College of Arts and Crafts, Oakland, Calif.	1907	33	8	13	468
California Institute of Technology, Pasadena, Calif.	1891	178	166	129	1,025
Carnegie Institute of Technology, Pittsburgh, Pa.	1900	300	260	87	4,034
Carthage College, Carthage, Ill.	1870	40	40	10	410
Cedar Crest College, Allentown, Pa.	1868	41	30	20	403
Chatham College, Pittsburgh, Pa.	1869	50	42	16	422

Institution					
The Chicago Theological Seminary, Chicago, Ill.	1855	36	27	22	116
Claremont Men's College, Claremont, Calif.	1947	35	20	14	327
College of Osteopathic Physicians and Surgeons, Los Angeles, Calif.	1914	309	39	"?"	344
Crozer Theological Seminary, Chester, Pa.	1867	*not stated*			63
De Paul University, Chicago, Ill.	1898	*restricted answer* [a]			6,320
Dickinson College, Carlisle, Pa.	1783	79	70	37	868
Drexel Institute of Technology, Philadelphia, Pa.	1894	253	198	105	5,917
Elizabethtown College, Elizabethtown, Pa.	1874	38	28	18	463
Elmhurst College, Elmhurst, Ill.	1871	59	41	17	725
Franklin and Marshall College, Lancaster, Pa.	1850	98	93	55	1,488
Garrett Biblical Institute, Evanston, Ill.	1855	21	20	18	431
Geneva College, Beaver Falls, Pa.	1883	59	36	? [b]	1,335
Gettysburg College, Gettysburg, Pa.	1832	75	65	37	1,183
Golden Gate College, San Francisco, Calif.	1901	84	13	0 [c]	1,715
Greenville College, Greenville, Ill.	1892	37	28	22	411
Haverford College, Haverford, Pa.	1833	65	55	31	482
Illinois College, Jacksonville, Ill.	1835	29	25	15	254
Illinois Institute of Technology, Chicago, Ill.	1892	*not stated*			6,309
Illinois Wesleyan University, Bloomington, Ill.	1853	83	60	35	701
Immaculate Heart College, Los Angeles, Calif.	1916	58	44	5	747
King's College, Wilkes-Barre, Pa.	1946	46	41	15	530
Knox College, Galesburg, Ill.	1837	68	68	41	772
Lafayette College, Easton, Pa.	1826	142	131	51	1,537
Lake Forest College, Lake Forest, Ill.	1857	59	48	12	638
La Salle College, Philadelphia, Pa.	1863	41 [d]	36 [d]	16 [d]	2,409
Lebanon Valley College, Annville, Pa.	1867	50	46	19	598

List of Institutions Studied (*continued*)

Name and Location	Charter	Teaching Staff* Total	Full-time	Tenure	Students †
Lehigh University, Bethlehem, Pa.	1866	restricted answer[a]			3,054
Lincoln University, Lincoln University, Pa.	1854	36	29	14	253
Loyola University of Los Angeles, Los Angeles, Calif.	1918	101	90	35	1,677
Lutheran Theological Seminary, Gettysburg, Pa.	1825	not stated[e]			132
Lutheran Theological Seminary, Philadelphia, Pa.	1893	12	10	9	203
MacMurray College, Jacksonville, Ill.	1863	49	40	30	425
McKendree College, Lebanon, Ill.	1834	25	25	20	330
Millikin University, Decatur, Ill.	1903	72	57	41	1,175
Mills College, Oakland, Calif.	1877	68	50	23	569
Moravian College, Bethlehem, Pa.	1863	48	37	15	584
Muhlenberg College, Allentown, Pa.	1848	51	47	23	670
Northwestern University, Evanston, Ill.	1851	1,594[f]	570[f]	450[f]	17,977
Occidental College, Los Angeles, Calif.	1887	103	73	45	1,336
The Pennsylvania State University, University Park, Pa.	1855	not stated			12,753
Pomona College, Claremont, Calif.	1887	102	88	22	1,017
Rockford College, Rockford, Ill.	1847	44	32	16	612
Roosevelt University, Chicago, Ill.	1945	195	92	68	3,254
St. Vincent College, Latrobe, Pa.	1870	21[g]	0[g]	1	661
Scripps College, Claremont, Calif.	1926	37	26	15	225
Seabury-Western Theological Seminary, Evanston, Ill.	1858	19	11	8	84
Stanford University, Stanford, Calif.	1885	1,325	556	200	7,288
Swarthmore College, Swarthmore, Pa.	1864	100	90	60	912

Temple University, Philadelphia, Pa.	1888	919	498	186	11,256
Thiel College, Greenville, Pa.	1870	30	28	14	375
United States Naval Postgraduate School, Monterey, Calif.	1909	97 h	97 h	83 h	522
University of California, Berkeley, Calif.	1868	5,050 j	3,400 j	1,650 j	33,382
University of Chicago, Chicago, Ill.	1890	757	735	392	6,234
University of Illinois, Urbana, Ill.	1868		not stated		21,164
University of Pennsylvania, Philadelphia, Pa.	1779	2,600 k	950 k	550 k	15,212
University of Pittsburgh, Pittsburgh, Pa.	1819	1,878	680	329	15,091
University of Redlands, Redlands, Calif.	1907	103	81	28	1,130
The University of Scranton, Scranton, Pa.	1888	restricted answer a			1,829
University of Southern California, Los Angeles, Calif.	1880	945	480	356	17,272
Valley Forge Military Academy, Wayne, Pa.	1928	restricted answer a			101
Westminster College, New Wilmington, Pa.	1852	81	66	25	1,015
Wheaton College, Wheaton, Ill.	1861	140	124	110	1,722
Wilkes College, Wilkes-Barre, Pa.	1933	82	56	24	1,514
Wilson College, Chambersburg, Pa.	1869	50	44	14	312

* From the replies to the questionnaire in 1955.

† From *Education Directory, 1954–55, Part 3* (U.S. Department of Health, Education, and Welfare; Office of Education, 1955).

a See explanation of "restricted answer" in the questionnaire reproduced below, Appendix B, p. 166.

b All except those serving their first year.

c Golden Gate College does not have tenure.

d There are in addition 39 full-time religious staff members not included in these figures.

e The reply indicates that the staff members have status in the ministry.

f The reply states "approximately."

g Does not include 16 full-time and 14 part-time teachers who are members of religious orders.

h Naval officers not included; civilians only.

j Estimate, from documents furnished by the University.

k "Approximately." "Full-time tenure teachers number approximately 550, and part-time 'tenure' teachers number at least this many or more."

B

The Questionnaire

TENURE LAW AND PRACTICE OF AMERICAN COLLEGES AND UNIVERSITIES

The purpose of this questionnaire is to obtain information and opinion relating to the law and practice of tenure acquisition and termination in colleges and universities of California, Illinois and Pennsylvania.

As an aid to full and free statement, the Project suggests the possibility of two kinds of answers:

1. *Unrestricted answers:* Answers not designated as restricted will be understood to be available for quotation and identifiable as to source and institution.

2. *Restricted answers:* The Project recognizes the complicated and ever-continuing public relations problem faced by every institution. Particularly, the chief administrator of a college or university may wish to communicate information or opinion but may hesitate to do so if his whole reply will be made public. We therefore suggest the possibility of restricted answers. Please feel free to indicate that an answer is not to be quoted, or a source or institution identified, without permission.

166

Please head your reply with the name of the reporting institution, the name and title of the reporting officer, and the date.

PART I. LEGAL STATUS OF INSTITUTION

1. *Public or private:* Is your institution controlled or financed by the state or municipality; does it have a private charter? Please describe.

2. *Selection of trustees:* How are trustees or regents selected, and for what terms?

3. *Controlling authority:* Under the statute, ordinance, or charter establishing your institution, who possesses the final responsibility for appointment and discharge of tenure teachers?

PART II. GOVERNING DOCUMENTS AND PROVISIONS

We request copies of the following documents or, if it is not feasible to supply a document, of the excerpts relevant to tenure: its meaning, and the standards and procedures governing appointment of teachers to tenure positions and governing termination of tenure appointments. If there are no such provisions or documents, please so state.

1. *Basic charter of the institution:* corporate charter; legislative enactment, municipal ordinance, etc.

2. *Implementing rulings, formal and informal:* trustee or regental rulings (such as statutes, by-laws, resolutions, operating manuals, statements of policy, expression of agreement with A.A.U.P. principles of academic freedom and tenure, decisions having precedent value, etc.); rulings by public officials such as attorneys general, superintendents of instruction, and other public officials.

3. *Institutional administrative rulings, formal, informal, and advisory:* regulations, rulings, statements, decisions, etc., by

167

officers or groups exercising formal or advisory authority (president, chancellor, provost, administrative or educational councils, etc.).

4. *Contract provisions:* contract forms including informal clauses contained in letters employing teacher or notifying non-tenure appointee of acquisition of tenure status. If there are relevant judicial or administrative decisions interpreting your contract terms, please give references.

5. *Faculty statements:* legislation, rulings, advisory statements of policy, etc., of faculty, faculty senate, etc.

6. *Other relevant documents and provisions.*

PART III. DEFINITION OF TENURE

1. *Official definition:* Please state the official definition of tenure in force at your institution. If there is no official definition, please so state.

2. *Informal definition:* If your experience and judgment as an administrator suggests divergence between the official definition of tenure and tenure in practice, please redefine it.

PART IV. ACQUISITION OF TENURE

In answering the following questions, please state whether your answer is based on the applicable rules, by-laws, etc., or whether it describes custom or practice not required by rules, by-laws, etc.

1. *Criteria:*

a) *Automatic:* Please state here (even if covered elsewhere) those standards which operate automatically, for example, tenure "by eighth annual appointment at the rank of instructor."

b) *Evaluative:* A statement of evaluative criteria or factors can only be a generalization about a host of individual decisions. But, from a number of such generalizations should come at least a picture of re-curring emphases. Accordingly, please state the criteria or factors which determine appointment or advance-ment to a tenure position.

2. *Procedure:* Please state the manner in which tenure is acquired at your institution, indicating the role of the faculty, department heads, administrative officials, and trustees in the process.

3. *Review of decision not to promote to tenure position:* Are there procedures under which a non-tenure appointee who has not been promoted to a tenure position may secure a review of this decision? If so, please describe.

PART V. TERMINATION OF TENURE
(other than by death or retirement)

1. *Criteria:* What are the criteria or reasons for terminating tenure? Are these criteria or reasons spelled out in applicable rules, by-laws, etc., or are they left for case to case develop-ment in interpreting a general clause, such as "good cause," etc.?

2. *Procedure:* Please list the rules, by-laws, etc., which prescribe the procedure to be followed in cases of termina-tion of tenure appointments, including provisions, if any, which pertain to informal conciliation, initiation of proceed-ings, pre-hearing procedures, requirements and character of hearing (confrontation, cross-examination, right to counsel, right to copy of record, etc.), designation of decisional author-ity, appellate procedures, and role of faculty, administration, and trustees, etc.

3. *Financial stringency provisions:* Please describe the pro-cedures and criteria intended to cover general staff curtail-ment or reductions in salary because of financial stringency, insofar as they affect tenure teachers.

PART VI. CASES

Please list cases relating to tenure acquisition or termination occurring at your institution within the past ten years and indicate whether a public or confidential record or report is available for study.

PART VII. STATISTICAL FRAMEWORK

1. Total teaching staff:
2. Total teaching staff, full time:
3. Total teaching staff on tenure:
4. Number of proceedings to terminate tenure which have been instituted on your campus during the past ten years:
5. Number of tenure teachers dismissed during the past ten years:
6. Number of tenure teachers granted full hearing and then dismissed during the past ten years:
7. Number of tenure teachers granted full hearing and then retained during the past ten years:
8. Number of tenure teachers who resigned after a question of tenure termination had been presented, during the past ten years:

The Project will be grateful for any general statement or critique you may wish to make.

C

Academic Freedom and Tenure
Statements of Principles*

Editor's Note: In 1915 a Committee on Academic Freedom and Academic Tenure of the American Association of University Professors formulated a statement on academic freedom and tenure, known as the 1915 Declaration of Principles, which was officially endorsed by the Association at its second Annual Meeting held in Washington, D.C., December 31, 1915 and January 1, 1916.

In 1925 the American Council on Education called a conference of representatives of a number of its constituent members, among them the American Association of University Professors, for the purpose of formulating a shorter statement. The statement formulated at this conference, known as the 1925 Conference Statement on Academic Freedom and Tenure, was endorsed by the Association of American Colleges in 1925 and by the American Association of University Professors in 1926.

* From the American Association of University Professors, *Bulletin*, 44: 290–293 (No. 1A, Spring, 1958).

In 1929 The American Association of University Professors formulated and endorsed a statement concerning academic resignations.

In 1940, following a series of joint conferences begun in 1934, representatives of the American Association of University Professors and of the Association of American Colleges agreed upon a restatement of the principles set forth in the 1925 Conference Statement. This restatement, known to the profession as the 1940 Statement of Principles on Academic Freedom and Tenure, was officially endorsed by the following organizations in the years indicated:

Association of American Colleges 1941
American Association of University Professors 1941
American Library Association (adapted for librarians) .. 1946
Association of American Law Schools 1946
American Political Science Association 1947
American Association of Colleges for Teacher Education [1] 1950
Association for Higher Education, National Education Association 1950
American Philosophical Association:
  Western Division 1952
  Eastern Division 1953
Southern Society for Philosophy and Psychology 1953

1940 Statement of Principles

The purpose of this statement is to promote public understanding and support of academic freedom and tenure and agreement upon procedures to assure them in colleges and universities. Institutions of higher education are conducted for the common good and not to further the interest of either

[1] Endorsed by predecessor, American Association of Teachers Colleges, in 1941.

the individual teacher [2] or the institution as a whole. The common good depends upon the free search for truth and its free exposition.

Academic freedom is essential to these purposes and applies to both teaching and research. Freedom in research is fundamental to the advancement of truth. Academic freedom in its teaching aspect is fundamental for the protection of the rights of the teacher in teaching and of the student to freedom in learning. It carries with it duties correlative with rights.

Tenure is a means to certain ends; specifically: (1) Freedom of teaching and research and of extramural activities, and (2) A sufficient degree of economic security to make the profession attractive to men and women of ability. Freedom and economic security, hence tenure, are indispensable to the success of an institution in fulfilling its obligations to its students and to society.

Academic Freedom

(a) The teacher is entitled to full freedom in research and in the publication of the results, subject to the adequate performance of his other academic duties; but research for pecuniary return should be based upon an understanding with the authorities of the institution.

(b) The teacher is entitled to freedom in the classroom in discussing his subject, but he should be careful not to introduce into his teaching controversial matter which has no relation to his subject. Limitations of academic freedom because of religious or other aims of the institution should be clearly stated in writing at the time of the appointment.

[2] The word "teacher" as used in this document is understood to include the investigator who is attached to an academic institution without teaching duties.

(c) The college or university teacher is a citizen, a member of a learned profession, and an officer of an educational institution. When he speaks or writes as a citizen, he should be free from institutional censorship or discipline, but his special position in the community imposes special obligations. As a man of learning and an educational officer, he should remember that the public may judge his profession and his institution by his utterances. Hence he should at all times be accurate, should exercise appropriate restraint, should show respect for the opinions of others, and should make every effort to indicate that he is not an institutional spokesman.

Academic Tenure

(a) After the expiration of a probationary period teachers or investigators should have permanent or continuous tenure, and their services should be terminated only for adequate cause, except in the case of retirement for age, or under extraordinary circumstances because of financial exigencies.

In the interpretation of this principle it is understood that the following represents acceptable academic practice:

(1) The precise terms and conditions of every appointment should be stated in writing and be in the possession of both institution and teacher before the appointment is consummated.

(2) Beginning with appointment to the rank of full-time instructor or a higher rank, the probationary period should not exceed seven years, including within this period full-time service in all institutions of higher education; but subject to the proviso that when, after a term of probationary service of more than three years in one or more institutions, a teacher is called to another institution it may be agreed in writing that his new appointment is for a probationary period of not more than four years, even though thereby the person's total

probationary period in the academic profession is extended beyond the normal maximum of seven years. Notice should be given at least one year prior to the expiration of the probationary period if the teacher is not to be continued in service after the expiration of that period.

(3) During the probationary period a teacher should have the academic freedom that all other members of the faculty have.

(4) Termination for cause of a continuous appointment, or the dismissal for cause of a teacher previous to the expiration of a term appointment, should, if possible, be considered by both a faculty committee and the governing board of the institution. In all cases where the facts are in dispute, the accused teacher should be informed before the hearing in writing of the charges against him and should have the opportunity to be heard in his own defense by all bodies that pass judgment upon his case. He should be permitted to have with him an adviser of his own choosing who may act as counsel. There should be a full stenographic record of the hearing available to the parties concerned. In the hearing of charges of incompetence the testimony should include that of teachers and other scholars, either from his own or from other institutions. Teachers on continuous appointment who are dismissed for reasons not involving moral turpitude should receive their salaries for at least a year from the date of notification of dismissal whether or not they are continued in their duties at the institution.

(5) Termination of a continuous appointment because of financial exigency should be demonstrably bona fide.

INTERPRETATIONS

At the conference of representatives of the American Association of University Professors and of the Association of

American Colleges on November 7–8, 1940, the following interpretations of the 1940 Statement of Principles on Academic Freedom and Tenure were agreed upon:

(1) That its operation should not be retroactive.

(2) That all tenure claims of teachers appointed prior to the endorsement should be determined in accordance with the principles set forth in the 1925 Conference Statement on Academic Freedom and Tenure.

(3) If the administration of a college or university feels that a teacher has not observed the admonitions of Paragraph (c) of the section on *Academic Freedom* and believes that the extramural utterances of the teacher have been such as to raise grave doubts concerning his fitness for his position, it may proceed to file charges under Paragraph (a) (4) of the section on *Academic Tenure*. In pressing such charges the administration should remember that teachers are citizens and should be accorded the freedom of citizens. In such cases the administration must assume full responsibility and the American Association of University Professors and the Association of American Colleges are free to make an investigation.

1925 Conference Statement [3]

[3] Superseded by the 1940 Statement of Principles on Academic Freedom and Tenure . . . [not reprinted here].

D

Recommended Institutional Regulations
on Academic Freedom and Tenure*

(Approved by Committee A on Academic Freedom and Tenure, August 4, 1957)

1. (a) The precise terms and conditions of every appointment to the faculty will be stated in writing and be in the possession of both the institution and the teacher before the appointment is consummated.

   (b) With the exception of temporary appointments for specifically limited terms, all full-time appointments to the rank of instructor or higher will be of two kinds: (1) probationary appointments, and (2) appointments with continuous tenure.

2. (a) Probationary appointments may be for one year or for other stated periods, subject to renewal; but the total probationary period will not exceed seven years, including previous full-time service with the rank of instructor or higher in other institutions of higher

* From a memorandum issued by the American Association of University Professors.

learning; *provided*, that in the case of a faculty member called from another institution it may be required that he serve in probationary status for a period not to exceed 4 years, even though thereby his total probationary period in the academic profession is extended beyond 7 years.

(b) Written notice that a probationary appointment is not to be renewed will be given to the faculty member in advance of the expiration of his appointment, according to the following minimum periods of notice: (1) at least 3 months before the end of his duties during the first academic year of faculty service in the institution, exclusive of a summer session; (2) not later than December 15 of the second academic year of such service, if the appointment expires at the end of that year; or, if a 2-year appointment terminates during an academic year, at least 6 months in advance of its termination; and (3) at least 12 months before the expiration of an appointment after more than 2 years in the institution. Notice of the terms and conditions of a renewal will in all cases be given at least 3 months before teaching duties terminate during the previous appointment, exclusive of a summer session.

3. Appointments will be with continuous tenure unless otherwise specified. Until retirement of the faculty member and subject to the procedure specified in Regulation 5, below, such an appointment is terminable by the institution only for adequate cause or on account of extraordinary financial emergencies, after not less than 12 months' notice to the faculty member.

4. If a member of the faculty desires to terminate an existing appointment, or to decline a renewal in the

absence of notice of non-renewal, he shall give notice not less than 3 months if his rank is instructor or assistant professor, and not less than 4 months if his rank is higher, before the end of his duties during an academic year exclusive of a summer session; but he may properly request a waiver of this requirement in case of hardship or in a situation where he would otherwise be denied substantial professional advancement.

5.   Termination for cause of a permanent appointee, dismissal of a faculty member during a limited appointment, or the non-renewal of a probationary appointment with less advance notice than that specified in these regulations shall be preceded by a statement of reasons and by opportunity to be heard by the tribunal or tribunals specified in Regulation 6. During the proceedings the faculty member will be permitted to have an advisor of his own choice, who may act as counsel. A full stenographic record of the hearing, if one is held, will be taken and made available to the parties concerned. If the faculty member's competence is in question, the testimony will include that of qualified faculty members from this or other institutions of higher education.

6.   [Here specify the tribunal or tribunals before which a hearing may be had pursuant to Regulation 5. A forthcoming joint statement of the Association of American Colleges and the American Association of University Professors will contain suggestions as to suitable tribunals.]

7.   Until the final decision upon termination of an appointment has been reached, the faculty member will be suspended only if immediate harm to him-

self or others is threatened by his continuance. If the appointment is terminated, the faculty member will receive his salary for at least the period of notice to which he is entitled under these regulations, and will be continued in his duties for that period unless his welfare or that of the institution requires that he be granted a leave of absence.

8. If a tenure appointment is terminated because of a financial emergency, the released faculty member's place will not be filled by a replacement within a period of two years, unless the released faculty member has been offered reappointment and has declined.

9. All members of the faculty are entitled to academic freedom as defined in the 1940 Statement of Principles of Academic Freedom and Tenure formulated by the Association of American Colleges and the American Association of University Professors. The pertinent provisions of this Statement are as follows:

(a) The teacher is entitled to full freedom in research and in the publication of the results, subject to the adequate performance of his other academic duties; but research for pecuniary return should be based upon an understanding with the authorities of the institution.

(b) The teacher is entitled to freedom in the classroom in discussing his subject, but he should be careful not to introduce into his teaching controversial matter which has no relation to his subject. Limitations of academic freedom because of religious or other aims of the institution should be clearly stated in writing at the time of the appointment.

(c) The college or university teacher is a citizen,

a member of a learned profession, and an officer of an educational institution. When he speaks or writes as a citizen, he should be free from institutional censorship or discipline, but his special position in the community imposes special obligations. As a man of learning and an educational officer, he should remember that the public may judge his profession and his institution by his utterances. Hence he should at all times be accurate, should exercise appropriate restraint, should show respect for the opinions of others, and should make every effort to indicate that he is not an institutional spokesman.

10. If a faculty member on probationary appointment alleges that a decision not to reappoint him is caused by considerations violative of academic freedom, his allegation shall be given preliminary consideration by the following faculty committee: [here designate, or specify the composition of, the committee]. If the committee concludes that there is probable cause for the faculty member's allegation, the matter shall be heard in the manner set forth in Regulation 5, except that the faculty member will be responsible for stating the grounds on which he bases his allegations and the burden of proof will rest upon him.

11. Administrative personnel who hold academic rank are subject to the foregoing regulations in their capacity as faculty members, and shall also have available, with reference to the termination of their appointments as administrators, the rights conferred in Regulation 10.

E

Statement on Procedural Standards
in Faculty Dismissal Proceedings*

Foreword

The following Statement on Procedural Standards in Faculty Dismissal Proceedings has been prepared by a joint committee representing the Association of American Colleges and the American Association of University Professors. It is intended to supplement the 1940 Statement of Principles on Academic Freedom and Tenure by providing a formulation of the "academic due process" that should be observed in dismissal proceedings. However, the exact procedural standards here set forth "are not intended to establish a norm in the same manner as the 1940 Statement of Principles of Academic Freedom and Tenure, but are presented rather as a guide. . . ." The committee members from the Association of American Colleges were President Louis T. Benezet (Colorado College), President Margaret Clapp (Wellesley College), and President Samuel B. Gould (Antioch College).

* From The American Association of University Professors, *Bulletin*, 44: 270–274 (No. 1A, Spring, 1958).

The other members were Professor Ralph F. Fuchs (Indiana University), Professor Quincy Wright (University of Chicago), and Professor Helen C. White (University of Wisconsin). . . . [The Statement was approved by the Association of American Colleges in January, 1958, and by the American Association of University Professors in April, 1958.]

Introductory Comments

Any approach toward settling the difficulties which have beset dismissal proceedings on many American campuses must look beyond procedure into setting and cause. A dismissal proceeding is a symptom of failure; no amount of use of removal process will help strengthen higher education as much as will the cultivation of conditions in which dismissals rarely if ever need occur.

Just as the board of control or other governing body is the legal and fiscal corporation of the college, the faculty are the academic entity. Historically, the academic corporation is the older. Faculties were formed in the Middle Ages, with managerial affairs either self-arranged or handled in course by the parent church. Modern college faculties, on the other hand, are part of a complex and extensive structure requiring legal incorporation, with stewards and managers specifically appointed to discharge certain functions.

Nonetheless, the faculty of a modern college constitute an entity as real as that of the faculties of medieval times, in terms of collective purpose and function. A necessary precondition of a strong faculty is that it have first-hand concern with its own membership. This is properly reflected both in appointments to and in separations from the faculty body.

A well-organized institution will reflect sympathetic understanding by trustees and teachers alike of their respective and complementary roles. These should be spelled out carefully in writing and made available to all. Trustees and faculty should understand and agree on their several functions in determining who shall join and who shall remain on the faculty. One of the prime duties of the administrator is to help preserve understanding of those functions. It seems clear on the American college scene that a close positive relationship exists between the excellence of colleges, the strength of their faculties, and the extent of faculty responsibility in determining faculty membership. Such a condition is in no wise inconsistent with full faculty awareness of institutional factors with which governing boards must be primarily concerned.

In the effective college, a dismissal proceeding involving a faculty member on tenure, or one occurring during the term of an appointment, will be a rare exception, caused by individual human weakness and not by an unhealthful setting. When it does come, however, the college should be prepared for it, so that both institutional integrity and individual human rights may be preserved during the process of resolving the trouble. The faculty must be willing to recommend the dismissal of a colleague when necessary. By the same token, presidents and governing boards must be willing to give full weight to a faculty judgment favorable to a colleague.

One persistent source of difficulty is the definition of adequate cause for the dismissal of a faculty member. Despite the 1940 Statement of Principles on Academic Freedom and Tenure and subsequent attempts to build upon it, considerable ambiguity and misunderstanding persist throughout higher education, especially in the respective conceptions of governing boards, administrative officers, and faculties concerning this matter. The present statement assumes that individual institutions will have formulated their own definitions of adequate cause for dismissal, bearing in mind the 1940 Statement and standards which have developed in the experience of academic institutions.

This statement deals with procedural standards. Those recommended are not intended to establish a norm in the same manner as the 1940 Statement of Principles on Academic Freedom and Tenure, but are presented rather as a guide to be used according to the nature and traditions of particular institutions in giving effect to both faculty tenure rights and the obligations of faculty members in the academic community.

Procedural Recommendations

1. Preliminary Proceedings Concerning the Fitness of a Faculty Member

When reason arises to question the fitness of a college or university faculty member who has tenure or whose term appointment has not expired, the appropriate administrative officers should ordinarily discuss the matter with him in personal conference. The matter may be terminated by mutual consent at this point; but if an adjustment does not result, a standing or *ad hoc* committee elected by the faculty and charged with the function of rendering confidential advice in such situations should informally inquire into the situation, to effect an adjustment if possible and, if none is effected, to determine whether in its view formal proceedings to consider his dismissal should be instituted. If the committee recommends that such proceedings should be begun, or if the president of the institution, even after considering a recommendation of the committee favorable to the faculty member, expresses his conviction that a proceeding should be undertaken, action should be commenced under the procedures which follow. Except where there is disagreement, a statement with reasonable particularity of the grounds proposed for the dismissal should then be jointly formulated by the president and the faculty committee; if there is disagreement, the president or his representative should formulate the statement.

2. Commencement of Formal Proceedings

The formal proceedings should be commenced by a communication addressed to the faculty member by the president of the institution, informing the faculty member of the statement formulated, and informing him that, if he so requests, a hearing to determine whether he should be removed from his faculty position on the grounds stated will be conducted by a faculty committee at a specified time and place. In setting the date of the hearing, sufficient time should be allowed the faculty member to prepare his defense. The faculty member should be informed, in detail or by reference to published regulations, of the procedural rights that will be accorded to him. The faculty member should state in reply whether he wishes a hearing and, if so, should answer in writing, not less than one week before the date set for the hearing, the statements in the president's letter.

3. Suspension of the Faculty Member

Suspension of the faculty member during the proceedings involving him is justified only if immediate harm to himself or others is threatened by his continuance. Unless legal considerations forbid, any such suspension should be with pay.

4. Hearing Committee

The committee of faculty members to conduct the hearing and reach a decision should either be an elected standing committee not previously concerned with the case or a committee established as soon as possible after the president's letter to the faculty member has been sent. The choice of members of the hearing committee should be on the basis of their objectivity and competence and of the regard in which they are held in the academic community. The committee should elect its own chairman.

5. Committee Proceeding

The committee should proceed by considering the statement of grounds for dismissal already formulated, and the faculty member's response written before the time of the hearing. If the faculty member has not requested a hearing, the committee should consider the case on the basis of the obtainable information and decide whether he should be removed; otherwise the hearing should go forward. The committee, in consultation with the president and the faculty member, should exercise its judgment as to whether the hearing should be public or private. If any facts are in dispute, the testimony of witnesses and other evidence concerning the matter set forth in the president's letter to the faculty member should be received.

The president should have the option of attendance during the hearing. He may designate an appropriate representative to assist in developing the case; but the committee should determine the order of proof, should normally conduct the questioning of witnesses, and, if necessary, should secure the presentation of evidence important to the case.

The faculty member should have the option of assistance by counsel, whose functions should be similar to those of the representative chosen by the president. The faculty member should have the additional procedural rights set forth in the 1940 Statement of Principles on Academic Freedom and Tenure, and should have the aid of the committee, when needed, in securing the attendance of witnesses. The faculty member or his counsel and the representative designated by the president should have the right, within reasonable limits, to question all witnesses who testify orally. The faculty member should have the opportunity to be confronted by all witnesses adverse to him. Where unusual and urgent reasons move the hearing committee to withhold this right, or where the witness cannot appear, the identity of the witness, as well as his statements, should nevertheless be disclosed to the faculty member. Subject to these safeguards, statements may when necessary be taken outside the hearing and reported to it. All of the evidence should be duly recorded. Unless special circumstances warrant, it should not be necessary to follow formal rules of court procedure.

6. Consideration by Hearing Committee

The committee should reach its decision in conference, on the basis of the hearing. Before doing so, it should give opportunity to the faculty member or his counsel and the representative designated by the president to argue orally before it. If written briefs would be helpful, the committee may request them. The committee may proceed to decision promptly, without having the record of the hearing transcribed, where it feels that a just decision can be reached by this means; or it may await the availability of a transcript of the hearing if its decision would be aided thereby. It should make explicit findings with respect to each of the grounds of removal presented, and a reasoned opinion may be desirable. Publicity concerning the committee's decision may properly be withheld until consideration has been given to the case by the governing body of the institution. The president and the faculty member should be notified of the decision in writing and should be given a copy of the record of the hearing. Any release to the public should be made through the president's office.

7. Consideration by Governing Body

The president should transmit to the governing body the full report of the hearing committee, stating its action. On the assumption that the governing board has accepted the principle of the faculty hearing committee, acceptance of the committee's decision would normally be expected. If the governing body chooses to review the case, its review should be based on the record of the previous hearing, accompanied by opportunity for argument, oral or written or both, by the principals at the hearing or their representatives. The decision of the hearing committee should either be sustained or the proceeding be returned to the committee with objections specified. In such a case the committee should reconsider, taking account of the stated objections and receiving new evidence if necessary. It should frame its decision and communicate it in the same manner as before. Only after study of the committee's reconsideration should the governing body make a final decision overruling the committee.

8. Publicity

Except for such simple announcements as may be required, covering the time of the hearing and similar matters, public statements about the case by either the faculty member or administrative officers should be avoided so far as possible until the proceedings have been completed. Announcement of the final decision should include a statement of the hearing committee's original action, if this has not previously been made known.

F

*Academic Due Process**

A Statement of Desirable Procedures
Applicable within Educational Institutions
in Cases Involving Academic Freedom

NOTE: This entire statement relates to *academic due process.* The *general legal* and *specific contractual questions* which may be involved in an academic freedom case are outside the scope of this discussion; these are questions of law which should be handled by the attorneys of the interested parties. Also excluded are the substantive criteria of academic freedom which are presented in other statements by the ACLU and other organizations.

Introductory Statement

AN ACADEMIC FREEDOM CASE in an American school, college, or university involves the rights and responsibilities of both the institution and the teacher, and the stake of the com-

---

* From a pamphlet published in 1954 by the American Civil Liberties Union; the text was prepared by that organization's national Academic Freedom Committee.

munity in its educational system. All of these interests are best guarded and served by the application of a clear, orderly and fair procedure to the adjudication of a case. Good procedure will minimize elements of personal conflict, and thereby reduce the bitterness which has so often left all parties to a controversy distrustful of the processes of justice and the reality of academic freedom. Good procedure in academic freedom cases has the same excellent power that legal due process has in the courts—it substitutes the rule of law for the rule of men.

Both the administration of an institution and the teacher should carefully consider the manner and degree in which an academic freedom case is publicized. It is true that if academic due process is not being observed, an appeal to public opinion may represent the only possible path to a just judgment. On the other hand, if fair procedures are being followed, excessive or intemperate publicizing should be avoided. Such publicizing, by the administration, may create community hostility which will affect (powerfully though irrelevantly) the real issues of competence and integrity. Such publicizing, by the teacher, may likewise result in subordination of the issues of competence and integrity; general community hostility may develop against an institution and its staff, or the particular teacher concerned may find himself required to offer defense against a new and perilously vague charge—that of "conduct unbecoming a teacher."

Warning must be given of an enormous range in the observance of due process. These pages set forth what the Academic Freedom Committee of the ACLU deems to be the best practice. This practice is observed by institutions which recognize the fact that democracy in the constitutional and political structure of the United States calls for an analogous democratic spirit in the American educational system. The best practice is not observed by those institutions which operate as retreats from reality, as victims to the whims and fears of the day, or as the preservers of their own vested interest in mere survival. Similarly, teachers will vary greatly. Academic due process will be observed by a responsible teacher who recognizes that his personal interest is linked to the interests of his institution and his community. Due process, unfortunately, will be misunderstood or abused by irresponsible and unworthy teachers. The warning should be repeated: the best academic due process is possible only when the institution and the teacher both believe that justice must be based upon order.

The principle embodied in the legal concept of confrontation should govern academic due process. The teacher should be informed of all the charges and all the evidence against him; he should have full opportunity to deny, to refute, and to rebut.

Finally, it is a fundamental principle of fairness that charges against a person are to be made the basis of action only when proven, and that the burden of proof rests upon those who bring them. Through the centuries, the courts have applied this principle in the formulation of legal due process, and it should operate with equal force in academic due process. The responsibility for applying this principle in the world of education rests primarily upon the governing board and administration of an institution. Plenitude of power imposes the obligation to keep every step in an academic freedom case totally untainted by the color of prejudgment.

A. Informal Conciliation

AN ACADEMIC FREEDOM CASE is likely to prove unfortunate for all, even if the best procedures are followed. The career and livelihood of the teacher are placed in danger. The reputation of the institution for fair dealing will be re-assessed by the educational world, sometimes without full knowledge of all the facts and issues. The community may become deeply divided between the camps of hypersensitive liberalism and truculent anti-intellectualism.

It is therefore especially desirable that the administrative authorities and the teacher (accompanied by an adviser) sit down together in a conciliatory session, confronting the charges and the evidence squarely, and sincerely attempting a solution of their common problems. A statement of the facts may clarify the situation; exposition of the teacher's point of view may persuade an administration not to review his competence and integrity; exposition of the administration's point of view may persuade a teacher to recognize his duty to cooperate with his institution, and to indicate how he may do so without sacrifice of principle. Any one of these developments, or all of them together, may yield a solution if the participants in the discussion are moved by genuine good will.

B. Procedure Preliminary to the Hearing

IN THE PERIOD OF PRELIMINARY ACTION, the administration and the teacher should assist each other in preparing the ground for an orderly and comprehensive hearing. The following actions are generally necessary:

1. The administration should present to the teacher a statement meeting the demands of the principle of confrontation, and embodying:

    a. Relevant legislation, board or trustee by-laws and rulings, administrative rulings, faculty legislation, etc.
    b. The charges in the particular case.
    c. A summary of the evidence upon which the charges are based, and a first list of witnesses to be called.
    d. The procedure to be followed, including a statement of the nature of the hearing body.
    e. A formal invitation to attend with adviser or counsel.

2. The teacher should select from among his colleagues a person of established position, wisdom, and judicial temper, who will act as his official academic adviser, or should select counsel to advise him on legal matters. He may, in his discretion, be assisted by both an academic adviser and a legal counselor. The teacher should inform the administration of the identity of his adviser or counsel and should obtain written agreement to his appearance on the teacher's behalf. (In what follows it is understood that when reference is made to the teacher, he is deemed to be acting under the advice of his adviser or counsel.)

3. The teacher should review the statement offered him by the administration (see "1" above); he may wish to supplement "1a" (governing rules), or to suggest modifications in "1b" (charges and "1d" (procedure); he should indicate the evidence by which he expects to refute the charges and should furnish a first list of witnesses he desires to call.

4. The administration and the teacher should, as completely as possible, at this point arrive at agreement on formulation of charges, governing rules, and procedure (if proper procedure has not previously been provided for). Such agreement will in no way prejudice, for either party, determination of the case on its merits. On the contrary, it will clarify the issues and make unnecessary at the hearing, or upon appeal, argument as to the *form* of the controversy, thereby permitting full attention to be given to matters of *substance*.

5. Communications, as a general rule, should be in writing, with copies retained. Oral discussion should be followed by an exchange of memoranda indicating the understanding which each party has of the conversation.

C. The Hearing; Tenure Teachers, Holders of Permanent Certificates, etc.

ACADEMIC DUE PROCESS provides for summary suspension or dismissal of a teacher holding tenure only when serious violation of law or immoral conduct is admitted, or proved before a competent court. All other charges should first be heard in formal hearing based upon the preliminary action outlined above in section "B." The hearing should take the following form:

1. The hearing committee should be a standing or special group of full-time teaching colleagues, democratically chosen by and representative of the teaching staff, and selected by pre-established rules. The administration should dissociate itself from those performing a judicial function at the hearing.

Note: The governance of some colleges and universities provides only for hearing committees established by the trustees or the president. The great majority of school system hearings are controlled by a hierarchic order of authority which culminates in the superintendent or board of education. Immediate and persistent efforts should be made by all teachers to bring such practices into conformity with the desirable procedure stated above in section "C-1."

2. The teacher should have the right to be present and to be accompanied by his personal adviser or his counsel throughout the hearing.

3. Both the teacher and the administration should have the right to present and examine witnesses and to cross-examine witnesses.

4. The administration should make available to the teacher such authority as it may possess to require the presence of witnesses.

5. The principle of confrontation should apply throughout the hearing.

6. A full record should be taken at the hearing; it should be made available in identical form and at the same time to the hearing group, the administration, and the teacher. The cost should be met by the institution.

7. The full text of the findings and conclusions of the hearing committee should be made available in identical form

and at the same time to the administration and the teacher. The cost should be met by the institution.

8. The hearing committee should promptly and forthrightly adjudicate the issues.

9. In the absence of a defect in procedure, the conclusions of the hearing committee should be taken as final by the administration and governing board in all matters relating to the teacher's competence and integrity.

10. But in the event of a finding unfavorable to a teacher, there should exist established procedures and channels for appeal, eventually leading to the ultimate authority responsible for the control of the institution.

D. The Hearing; Non-Tenure Teachers, Holders of Temporary Certificates, etc.

AMERICAN EDUCATIONAL PRACTICE permits great fluidity in the testing of teachers as to their permanent usefulness in a particular institution. This experimental phase of a teacher's career is wisely characterized by a minimum of formal judgment; teachers come and go without recorded praise or blame. Furthermore, non-tenure appointments often fall within the marginal area of an institution's educational and financial program; the dropping of a teacher may have no bearing whatsoever upon his professional capacity. But, although non-retention does not necessarily raise an academic freedom issue, such an issue may be present in non-retention. For example, improper consideration may have been given to non-academic matters, such as a teacher's race, or his religious or political beliefs and associations. Such improper consideration is a violation of academic freedom and the non-tenure teacher is entitled to all the protections of academic due process. (It is understood, of course, that an institution of publicly declared faith may limit employment to teachers of that faith. Similarly, an institution of special function may establish particular criteria; for example, a school for young girls might properly hire only women.)

Action in non-tenure academic freedom cases should take this general form:

1. If the non-tenure teacher believes that improper considerations have unmistakably affected the decision not to retain him, he should, with appropriate advice, determine whether he can assemble adequate proof in support of his contention.

2. The teacher should decide whether he is willing to hazard the possible disclosure of professional weaknesses he may have displayed at an early point in his career.

3. If his decisions under "1" and "2" are positive, he should request an opportunity for informal conciliation as set forth in section "A," above.

4. If such informal conciliation is denied, or unsuccessful, he should then request a formal hearing, and submit a written waiver of the traditional right of non-tenure teachers to non-disclosure of the grounds upon which they have been released.

5. The administration should then grant to the teacher the entire procedure for adjudication set forth above in sections "B" and "C."

Index

Bylaws, as part of teacher's contract, 83-85

Byse, Clark, 103, 117

California, University of, 13, 15, 18, 23-26

California College of Arts and Crafts, 13, 15

California Institute of Technology, 11

Cardozo, Benjamin N., 127

Carnegie Institute of Technology, 11, 128

Cause, as tenure-termination criterion, 44, 45

Chafee, Zechariah, Jr., 5, 74, 103, 104, 114, 119, 125

Chambers, M. M., 80, 83

Chandler, Gardner & Williams, Inc. v. *Reynolds*, 113

Charges, in tenure termination, 54, 56, 104, 148

Charter provisions:
authorize discharge at will, 79-82, 105
quoted, 79-80

Chatham College, 18-19, 79

Cheyney, Edward Potts, 127

Chicago, University of, 14, 15, 16, 17, 67, 82, 115

Chicago Theological Seminary, 13, 15, 33

Church-related colleges and universities, *see* Denominational colleges and universities

Church representatives, college trustees as, 151

Claremont Men's College, 14, 15, 31-32

Clark v. *Wild Rose Special School Dist.*, 122

Coats v. *General Motors Corp.*, 113

Cobb v. *Howard University*, 80, 82, 83, 86

College of Osteopathic Physicians and Surgeons, 11

Colleges, *see American colleges and universities by name*

Colorado School of Mines v. *Neighbors*, 102

Commager, Henry Steele, 2

Committee:
ad hoc, in tenure termination, 58, 60
faculty, in tenure acquisition, 35, 36, 38, 39, 41
faculty, in tenure termination, 51, 58-59, 60, 62-63
faculty, reviewing denial of tenure, 43
governing board, in tenure termination, 59
standing, in tenure termination, 58, 60
see also Joint committee

"Common law" of academic affairs, 135

Communist party membership, as tenure-termination criterion, 98

Conant, James Bryant, 142-143

Conciliation and informal adjustment, 53-56

Confrontation of witnesses, 60-62, 118, 119, 149

Consideration, in tenure contract, 92-94

Constitution, faculty tenure plan in, 77

Constitutional protection of academic freedom, 76, 119

Contempt of court, nonperformance of contract as, 73

Contract:
breach of, 72-74, 78-94, 108
consideration in tenure, 92-94
damages for breach of, 72-73
freedom of v. academic freedom, 137
lifetime employment, compared to tenure contracts, 93
personal service, remedy for breach, 73-74
power of college or university to make, 79-82
"satisfaction" of party as term of, 113
specific performance, 73

Enforcement, legal (*cont.*)
  limitations of, 74, 136-137
  obstacles to in charters of col-
    leges and universities, 79-
    82, 105
  tenure plans should facilitate,
    136-137
  of tenure, insubstantial, 136
Equitable remedies, for wrongful
  dismissal, 73-74
European colleges and universities,
  124, 154
Evaluative criteria, for acquisition
  of tenure, 28-34, 69, 141
Evidence in tenure-termination
  proceedings, 56, 60, 61, 64
Exigencies, financial, as tenure-termination criterion, 49-51
External actions, as tenure-termination criterion, 104, 142-144

Faculty:
  committee of:
    role in tenure acquisition, 35-
      39, 43
    role in tenure termination, 51,
      58, 60, 62-63, 147-148
    delegation of decisional power
      to, 124-127
    role in tenure acquisition, 38-41,
      69, 141-142
    recommendation re, 142
    role in tenure termination, 58-
      59, 63, 68, 110, 121, 124-127,
      145-148, 156
    recommendation re, 148-149
Faculty-administration (governing
  board) committee, *see* Joint
  committee
Faculty–governing board committee, *see* Joint committee
Faculty member:
  as institutional spokesman, avoid-
    ance of impression of, 138-
    139
  obligations of, 138-139
  see also Teacher
Failure in institutional relationship,
  as tenure-termination criterion,
  47-48

Finality clauses, 110-115, 136
Financial exigencies, as tenure-ter-
  mination criterion, 49-51
Financial problems, as cause for
  tenure denial, 42
Fletcher, William M., 125
Formal hearing in tenure termina-
  tion, 56-67
Formal tenure plan, 9, 134-136
Franklin and Marshall College, 11
Freedom of expression, compared
  to academic freedom, 2
"Freehold" in teaching position, 78
Full professor, automatic tenure to,
  13-15
Fuller v. *De Paul University,* 98

Garrett Biblical Institute, 11
Gellhorn, Walter, 117
Geneva College, 11, 12, 79
Gettysburg College, 11, 79
Golden Gate College, 10, 18
Governing board:
  authority reduced by judicial re-
    view, 109
  composition of, 151
  final authority, in tenure-termi-
    nation cases, 136, 146
  qualifications of, 152
  removal of member by faculty,
    154
  rule-making power, 116
  and tenure acquisition, 35, 37-38,
    41, 43
  and tenure termination, 59, 68,
    108-109, 111, 136, 149, 150
  see also Board of trustees *and*
    Trustee
Governing board–administration-
  faculty committee, *see* Joint
  committee
Government of colleges and universities:
  European v. American traditions,
    124
  role of faculty, 145
Greenville College, 11, 32-33, 48
Griswold, Erwin N., 130
Groves v. *Carolene Products Co.,*
  112

Moral turpitude, as tenure-termination criterion, 46, 47, 104
Moravian College, 11
Muhlenberg College, 14, 15, 16, 82-83
Murdock, Appellant from a Decree of the Visitors of the Theological Institution in Phillips Academy, 95-96, 108, 114
Murdock v. Phillips Academy, 95, 108, 120
Mutuality of obligation and tenure, 92-94

Nathanson, Nathaniel L., 117
Natural law, justification for due process, 117
Neglect of duty, as tenure-termination criterion, 45, 80, 104
Nevada, University of, 98-101
Nonreappointment, appeal from, 41-43
Northwestern University, 13, 16, 17, 80
Notice:
as due process requirement, 117-118, 130
in tenure-termination procedures, necessity for, 124
Notice and hearing, *see* Hearing

Oaths, loyalty, 76
O'Brian, John Lord, 130
Occidental College, 14, 15, 16
Opinions of teacher, as tenure-termination criterion, 101-102, 103, 104
Osteopathic Physicians and Surgeons, College of, 11

Panama Refining Co. v. Ryan, 127
Paramount Publix Corp., In re, 81
Parker, Isaac, 96, 101
Patton v. Babson Statistical Organization, Inc., 112
Pennsylvania, University of, 13, 15, 110, 126-127
Pennsylvania Female College, 79
see also Chatham College
Pennsylvania State University, 11

People ex rel. Kelsey v. New York Post-Graduate Medical School and Hospital, 83, 90
Personal service contract, remedy for breach, 73-74
Peters v. Hobby, 123
Physical incapacity, as tenure-termination criterion, 47, 79
Pittsburgh, University of, 14, 15, 16, 80, 124-125
Podell, Lawrence, 158
Political disloyalty, as tenure-termination criterion, 46
Pomona College, 13
Posin v. State Board of Higher Education, 81-82, 125
Practice, tenure recognized in, 77
Practice of tenure without official commitment, 17-28
Prejudice, disqualification for, 129
President:
delegation of power to, 128-129
dismissal of teachers by, charter provision for, 80
disqualification for bias or prejudice, 129
final decisional power, 128-129
importance of in tenure termination, 109
relationship to governing board, 109
role in tenure acquisition, 35, 37, 38, 40, 41
role in tenure termination, 59, 63, 68, 146
Private colleges and universities:
breach of contract by, 72-74, 78-94, 108
judicial review of tenure termination in, 107-117
teacher's legal remedies against, compared with public, 72-74
Probationary period:
before acquiring tenure, 9-28, 139-141
"consideration" of tenure after, 141
tenure after service of, recommendation re, 139-141
see also Assistant professor, Asso-

INDEX

Richardson, State ex rel., v. *Board of Regents*, 72, 78, 98-103, 106, 107-108, 109
Rockford College, 14, 80, 115
Roosevelt University, 14, 15, 16, 17, 34, 55-56, 57, 63, 64, 66, 67, 83
Rose and Frank Co. v. *Crompton Bros., Ltd.*, 86
Royster Guano Co. v. *Hall*, 93
Rules:
  breach of, as tenure-termination criterion, 115-117
  governing board's power to change, 115-117
Rutledge, Wiley B., 82, 84, 94

St. Vincent College, 14, 48
Salaries, reduction of due to financial exigencies, 51
"Satisfaction" of a contracting party, 113
Scher v. *School District*, 108
Schilling, Bernard N., 42
School City v. *Sigler*, 116
Schulz v. *Knights of Maccabees of the World*, 127
Schwartz, Bernard, 117
Scope of review, 105-114
Scripps College, 13, 15, 16
Seabury-Western Theological Seminary, 13, 15
Security against dismissal, tenure defined as, 2
Seminaries, theological, *see* Denominational colleges and universities
Separation of prosecution and adjudication, in tenure termination, 60, 62-64, 128-129
Service to community and nation, as tenure criteria, 29
Shannon, George Pope, 140
Shaughnessy v. *United States*, 118
Simpson, Sidney P., 74
Sittler v. *Board of Control*, 91, 125
Social forces, interaction with academic traditions, 151
Southern California, University of, 13, 15, 16, 17

Specific performance, 73-74, 136
Spooner v. *Reserve Life Insurance Co.*, 86
Standards, for tenure acquisition and termination, *see* Criteria
Standing committee, as tenure-termination hearing group, 58, 60
Stanford University, 13, 30-31, 80
State ex rel. Anderson v. *Brand*, 93
State ex rel. Board of Directors v. *Preston*, 122
State ex rel. Bourgeois v. *Board of Supervisors*, 113
State ex rel. Howard v. *Ireland*, 122
State ex rel. Keeney v. *Ayers*, 72, 78, 83, 92, 93, 116
State ex rel. Richardson v. *Board of Regents*, 72, 78, 98-103, 106, 107-108, 109
State-financed colleges and universities:
  included in study, 7
  judicial review of tenure termination, 105-108
  legal enforcement of tenure in, 71, 73, 78
  tenure plans as sublegislation, 71
State teachers colleges, excluded from study, 7
"Statement of Principles," 1940, AAUP-AAC, 171-176
"Statement on Procedural Standards in Faculty Dismissal Proceedings," 182-189
Status of teacher, recommendation re legal protection of, 138
Statute, protection of tenure by, not recommended, 121
Statute of Frauds, and informal tenure plans, 91
Statutes of colleges and universities, violation of as termination criterion, 115-117
Steen v. *Board of Civil Service Comm'rs.*, 123
Stene, Edwin O., 2, 114
Stevens, Robert S., 125

209

INDEX

Stevens v. *G. L. Rugo & Sons, Inc.*, 93, 113
Stewart, George R., 26
Students, undermining faith and morals of, as tenure-termination criterion, 48
Subpoena power, in tenure-termination procedures, 65-66
Subversive conduct, as tenure-termination criterion, 46
Summers, Clyde W., 108, 114, 119, 129
Suspension, during tenure-termination proceeding, 150
Sutherland, Arthur E., 76
Swarthmore College, 11
Sweezy v. *New Hampshire*, 76
Sylvan Crest Sand & Gravel Co. v. *United States*, 92

Taylor, Harold, 103
Teacher:
  acquisition of tenure, *see* Acquisition of tenure
  criteria for dismissal, *see* Criteria, for termination of tenure
  dismissal:
    as breach of contract, 72, 78-116
    charter provisions re, 79
    court decisions on, 80-116
    injunction against, 74
    judicial review of, 95-116
    legal remedies, 71-94
    money damages, 72-74, 80-81, 95
    reinstatement, 72-74, 79-81, 138
  and employee, compared, 154-155
  as expert, 156-157
  as institutional spokesman, avoidance of impression, 138-139
  obligations, 138-139
  reinstatement, 72-74, 79-81, 138
  resignation, 92-93, 138-139
  responsibilities re, recommendations re, 138-139
  status, recommendation re, 138
  suspension of, during tenure-termination proceeding, 150
  values of, 152
  differ from those of trustees, 151-154
Temple University, 14, 15, 16, 92-93, 128
Tenure plans:
  dismissal in violation of, legal remedies for, 71-94
  documentary proof of, 90-91
  formal, 9
    absence of, 135
  legal problems of, 77-130
  percentage officially adopted, 10
  of state-financed colleges and universities, as sublegislation, 72, 105
  variety of, 133
  written v. unwritten, 134-136
Tenure termination, *see* Termination of tenure
Term of service as tenure requirement, *see* Probationary period
"Term-rank," acquisition of tenure, 13-15
Termination of tenure:
  as breach of contract, 72, 78-116
  broad charter provisions for, 79-82
  control by presidents, 109
  court decisions on, 80-116
  criteria, *see* Criteria, for termination of tenure
  judicial review of, 95-116
  legal remedies for wrongful, 71-95, 138
  procedure:
    appeal to president or governing board, 68, 149
    confrontation, 60-62, 118-119, 149
    constituency of hearing committee, 57-60, 148
    copy of record, 66-67
    counsel, 63-64, 149
    cross-examination, 60-61, 64-65, 118, 119, 123, 149
    informal adjustment and conciliation, 53-56, 148

BYSE, CLARK

Tenure in American higher education: plans, practices, and the law, by Clark Byse and Louis Joughin. Ithaca, N. Y., Cornell University Press [1959]

212 p. 22 cm. (Cornell studies in civil liberty)

1. College teachers—Tenure—U. S.   I. Joughin, George Louis, joint author.   II. Title.

LB2334.B95   378.12   59–10438 ‡

Library of Congress